The New York Times

SUNDAY CROSSWORD PUZZLES VOLUME 37
50 Sunday Puzzles from the Pages of *The New York Times*

Edited by Will Shortz

ST. MARTIN'S GRIFFIN ❧ NEW YORK

THE NEW YORK TIMES SUNDAY CROSSWORD PUZZLES VOLUME 37.
Copyright © 2011 by The New York Times Company.
All rights reserved. Printed in China. For information, address
St. Martin's Press, 175 Fifth Avenue, New York, NY 10010.

www.stmartins.com

All of the puzzles that appear in this work were originally published in
The New York Times from July 2, 2006, to June 17, 2007.
Copyright © 2006, 2007 by The New York Times Company.
All rights reserved. Reprinted by permission.

ISBN 978-0-312-64549-6

First Edition: November 2011

10   9   8   7   6   5   4   3   2

The New York Times

SUNDAY CROSSWORD PUZZLES VOLUME 37

The New York Times

SMART PUZZLES

Presented With Style

ACROSS

1 Some radio dispatches, for short
5 Album feature
10 ___ Popular
15 Small handful
19 "George of the Jungle" elephant
20 Historic symbol whose shape can be found hidden in this completed puzzle
22 ___'acte
23 Southern side?
24 Made better
25 French noodle product?
26 Shot by a doctor
28 1776–1876: Abbr.
29 Guitarlike Japanese instruments
31 Better set
32 Hypodermics
34 Alexander Hamilton's place, informally
35 It's filled with bills
36 Allegro ___ (music direction)
38 Grps.
40 Prefix with dermis
41 Lateral lead-in
42 Takes power away from
46 Henpeck
47 Bard's nightfall
48 Shavings
51 TV canine
52 Old washing machine feature
56 34th U.S. pres.
57 Opposite of blow up
59 "I beg to differ!"
61 Neat
63 Stage elevator
64 Bighearted one
65 Out
66 Ones making amphibious landings?
68 They go all out at beauty shops
69 Center of Florida?
72 Coulter who wrote "Godless: The Church of Liberalism"
73 Mention
77 Kind of I.R.A.
78 Broadcasts
81 Big bird
82 U.S. atty. gen. in 1962
83 In a Weird Al Yankovic song, he "looks like a Muppet, but he's wrinkled and green"
84 Get-up-and-go
85 Certain fungus
86 Book before James: Abbr.
87 "Cool" amount
88 Saturate, in dialect
89 "Sweet as apple cider" girl
90 Cheesehead
91 Ballantine, e.g.
92 First group of invitees
95 "Consider it done!"
98 More fit
100 Moving away from the sides
102 German auto pioneer Gottlieb
103 Carpentry supplies
104 Like Saturn
105 Skin cleanser component
106 In the middle of
107 Not dis
110 Whirler
112 Comedy shtick
113 Twisty turn
116 Within reach
121 Savory French appetizers
125 "Tell me about it"
126 Much-photographed White House area
127 Accent
128 Misses the wake-up call

DOWN

1 Like many T's and P's
2 Emergency calling plan
3 Image that appears with the 20-Across on an old half dollar
4 Go over the limit?
5 Groups that run
6 Olympic officials
7 Still snoring
8 Actor Gibson
9 Like a Rolls-Royce
10 Talking Heads co-founder David
11 Legal org.
12 Pulls in
13 Baseballers' wear
14 Graybeards
15 Houdini's real name
16 Longtime setting for 20-Across
17 Things needed around dictators
18 High reputes
21 Ornament that may be worn with sandals
27 Org. with operations
30 Pulls
32 Original ___
33 Hang
37 Mozart's birthplace: Abbr.
39 From Phila. to Miami
43 Hard stuff
44 Repeated phrase in Martin Luther King Jr.'s "I Have a Dream" speech
45 Like a juggernaut
48 Elapse
49 Polished off
50 Fraudulent contestant
53 Welcome, as the new year
54 Green: Prefix
55 Check over
58 Hat, slangily
59 Top-secret grp.
60 Sounds of woe
62 It often gets glossed over
66 Airport area
67 Previously recorded
70 Dish prepared in a skillet
71 Rutabagas, e.g.
74 Starr and others
75 Japanese noodle product
76 Temple with curved roofs
78 Put forward
79 Muslim leader
80 Call
93 Series
94 Rocks
96 June honorees
97 Author Deighton
98 Direct contact
99 Routine
101 Domestic Old World birds
103 Creme-filled chocolate treats
107 Talking point?
108 I.R.A. part: Abbr.
109 "There's gold in them ___ hills!"
111 Oil producer
112 Afrikaner
113 Earth, to Mahler
114 Flight segment
115 Payroll dept. ID's
117 Follower of Benedict?
118 Pastoral cry
119 P.O. box item
120 Comics shriek
121 Granada gold
122 Natl. Novel Writing mo.
123 British verb ending
124 It may follow you

by Elizabeth C. Gorski

2 Kneecaps

ACROSS

1 Makes sticky
7 Old Spanish gold
14 Plato dubbed her "the tenth Muse"
20 Turkey's highest peak
21 Buddy
22 Served the drinks
23 It means "strained" in drink names
24 Author of "The Fall of the Horse of Usher"?
26 Mad cap?
28 Dudgeon
29 "Dinner and a Movie" airer
30 Prefix with friendly
31 Caring grp.
32 Coal byproduct
33 Hard slog
35 Arthur and others
36 It may be legally beaten
37 Accomplish flawlessly
39 Essential part
40 American representative to France during the Revolutionary War
41 Love hate?
46 Iron man?
49 If things go well
50 Cry with a pompom
51 What golf pencils lack
54 Brand of craft knives
55 Cubes
59 Unable to make "Ocean's Thirteen," maybe?
62 Actress Olin
63 Break down
64 Professionals' earnings
65 From scratch
68 Exotic means of suicide
69 Brewed beverages
71 Organ that can perform martial arts moves?
78 Writing set?
81 Alprazolam, more familiarly
82 Femme fatale, often
83 Progressive ___
84 Quick-change artists?
86 1983 Nicholas Gage book
87 Ex-wife's refrain?
93 Products with earbuds
94 2004 spinoff show
95 Lip-puckering
96 Long ride?
99 Recording device
100 Blue
101 All for
104 "___ dien," motto of the Prince of Wales
105 Specialist M.D.
106 Reason to retire
107 Monstrous bird of myth
108 How a diaper is removed?
111 Cry to a lunch sandwich before it's eaten?
115 Set off
116 Arctic natives
117 "Eureka!"
118 "Is this a ___ which I see before me": Macbeth
119 Salary after deductions
120 Sequoias and Siennas
121 Whiles away

DOWN

1 Angel
2 Beethoven's Third
3 Hurry on horseback
4 River through Kazakhstan
5 Jotted down
6 Alien
7 Three-sided blade
8 Mubarak's predecessor
9 Company with the motto "A Business of Caring"
10 Old carrier name
11 Have the gumption
12 ___ roll
13 Roman Helios
14 Catalyst
15 Top-notch
16 Spot early on?
17 Able to change shape
18 Unwanted plant in farmyards
19 Spacecraft orbiting Mars
25 Mislead and then some
27 Hook worm
33 Pan coating
34 Off-color
35 Hebrew for "house of God"
38 Wahine accessory
39 Very, to Verdi
40 Horror movie figure, informally
41 British bludgeon
42 Year that Spenser's "The Faerie Queene" was published
43 Set of rings?
44 Food item that can be soft or hard
45 Historic Swiss canton
46 Prepare to give what you received?
47 Brooks Robinson, for 23 years
48 Secure tightly, with "down"
52 Lament
53 Chooses to leave
55 Units of force
56 Late wake-up call?
57 Seemingly not there
58 Ancient manuscripts
60 Black layer found in Morbier cheese
61 Put dishes away
66 Stretch (out)
67 Pull ahead yet further
70 Small suit
72 Left
73 Actress Bates
74 Ending with sever or suffer
75 ___ avis
76 It'll turn you around
77 In a proper manner
79 Shaw's "___ and the Man"
80 Research center
84 On-the-water front
85 Wildean quality
87 Drug taken mostly by kids
88 Inferior imitator
89 Pack up and go
90 Deplane dramatically
91 Common street name
92 Nero Wolfe's obsession
96 Not harmful
97 Together
98 They're rounded up in a roundup
100 Punk
101 Utah County seat
102 Big name in reference books
103 ___ vincit amor
107 Nino who composed the music for "The Godfather"
108 Scold severely
109 Feedbag's fill
110 "Splendor in the Grass" writer
112 Currency of Laos
113 It may come straight from the horse's mouth
114 "Now the truth comes out!"

by Patrick Berry

ACROSS

1 Pelvic
6 P.M. times
10 Fast feline
14 They don't do Windows, as a rule
19 Sheryl Crow's "All I ___ Do"
20 Goggle
21 City south of Moscow
22 Lollygag
23 EVIL BRAT IN THERE
26 Muchachas: Abbr.
27 Part of the refrain before "hey hey hey" in a 1969 #1 song
28 ___ League
29 Absorbed
30 CANNY OLDER AUTHOR
34 Notches, usually
38 Honk
39 Frown
40 School for King's Scholars
41 Not manual
42 Signs
44 Passers, briefly
47 TO APPEAR ON ELBA, NON?
52 Diminutive suffix
53 Nevada county
54 Sharper
55 P.O. items
56 1940's–50's All-Star Johnny
57 Old cars with 389 engines
58 Secretary of state before Shultz
59 Diet doctor
61 EAGER TO USE LYRICAL MOLD
68 Benedict XV's successor
69 Vault
70 Narc tail?
71 Playfully roguish
72 Jason ___, longtime Denver Bronco
73 Touch
76 Recipe instruction
79 Sci-fi drug
80 SEEN ALIVE? SORRY, PAL!
84 Co. founded by Perot
85 Old-fashioned contraction
86 Good buddy
87 Abbey area
88 Like some Fr. nouns
89 God whose wife had hair of finely spun gold
90 Storyteller's challenge
93 EVER THE CRISP HERO
98 Taos sight
99 Picnic hamperer
100 "Clever thinking"
105 Esther of "Good Times"
106 I VALUE NICER ROLE
109 Affaire
110 Some wings
111 B'way showing
112 Part of a platform
113 Carryalls
114 Dying words?
115 It's usually slanted
116 Pete ___, 1970's–80's General Motors chief

DOWN

1 "Bingo!"
2 Source of basalt
3 ___ uproar
4 Tolstoy heroine
5 Short break
6 Operatives
7 Al ___ (Mideast group)
8 Philosopher Mo-___
9 Sun. talk
10 Herculean literary character?
11 Concentrated, in a way
12 Peach ___
13 Cask contents
14 "I give up"
15 St. Stephen, in the Bible
16 Soviet cooperative
17 One doing heavy lifting
18 Meth.
24 Hopper
25 Nocturnal animal: Var.
29 Start of a refusal
31 Part of an instrument measuring fluid pressure
32 Kind of blade
33 Pirates and Cards
34 Kind of diagram in logic
35 Dog command
36 Word before and after "against"
37 "Wheel of Fortune" buy
41 Industrious one
42 Some nerve
43 Pulitzer-winning critic Jefferson
44 Dennis of "The Alamo"
45 Hip-hop jewelry, in short
46 Pick up
48 Glove material
49 Potentially dangerous strain
50 Boot
51 Winged
56 Their tips turn up
57 Wax rhapsodic
58 Short flight
59 Race of Norse gods
60 Group of three
61 Rush
62 Was on
63 Goos
64 Texas hold 'em announcement
65 Catalytic converter?
66 Temple tender
67 Flight maneuver
72 Boot
73 Pergola
74 Baseball Hall-of-Famer Bobby
75 Dad's namesake: Abbr.
76 "Kubla Khan" river
77 First name in 50's TV
78 Salon supplies
80 Amazon.com and others
81 Stop from running, maybe
82 One-seeded fruit, botanically
83 Parked oneself
88 1959 #1 hit by the Fleetwoods
89 Craving
90 Start a drive
91 Like Ford's logo
92 Garment size
93 1980's–90's New York governor
94 Spartan serf
95 Toothbrush handle?
96 1945 Physics Nobelist Wolfgang ___
97 Madrid month
98 Something to fall on
101 Composer Charles
102 Force
103 Clown shoe width
104 Culture
106 August person
107 "Wait Wait . . . Don't Tell Me!" network
108 Bus. driver?

by Ashish Vengsarkar

ACROSS

1 Corp. honcho
5 Some Filipinos
10 Starter's need
13 TV alien
17 Storyteller of Samos
19 Virtuous sort
20 Duration of many a TV show
23 Wine that causes incoherent talk?
25 Vietnamese city painted in soothing colors?
26 Pseudopod formers
27 Capital on the Mississippi
29 "Missed it!"
30 Literary governess
32 Girl's name that's a Texas county seat
33 Second word of many limericks
34 What a dummy!
37 French priest born in early July?
41 Worry, it's said
45 Calif. hub
46 Not quite right?
48 Mint hardware
49 Fillet
51 Poppy derivative
53 W.W. II-era enlistee
55 They're trident-shaped
57 Dries, in a way
58 Popular British society magazine
59 Steamed
61 Authorize
63 Life of ___
64 Monologist of note
65 Start of Montana's motto
66 Source of iron
67 Defeats regularly, in sports lingo
69 Cracker spread that's a little sparse on top?
74 Shook down
75 Game with matchsticks
76 Yearbook sect.
77 Brownie, e.g.
78 ___' Pea
80 Dasher, to Dancer
83 Gave in
84 Haberdashery item
87 Put out
88 It melts in your mouth
90 Journal add-on?
91 Attire
92 Bungled, with "up"
94 Common order, with "the"
96 Bit of sports news
98 Foreign exchange option
99 Kind of engr.
100 Discontinued investigative series?
103 Chanson de ___
105 Some choristers
107 Spot in a Manilow tune
108 Ad headline
110 Centers of squares, maybe
113 Brute
116 Deli offering
120 Expert in ornamental fabrics?
122 Rate at which a personnel manager works?
124 Orchard starter
125 Cream
126 "Not my problem!"
127 1940's first lady

128 Rehabilitated, in a way
129 Boxer-turned-actor
130 Ring

DOWN

1 Jumper, briefly
2 Enlarge, in a way
3 Salinger dedicatee
4 Lamenting one
5 Common Internet letters
6 Bireme gear
7 Sidesplitter
8 With no guarantees
9 Was of use to
10 Make it big
11 ___ corda (music marking)
12 Trojan War sage
13 Like pure gold
14 Dept. of Labor div.
15 Romp
16 Place for a pad
18 After-school arrangements
21 Punished, in a way, in the Bible
22 Fair-hiring org.
24 U.S. ally since '48
28 Green
31 Old five-franc coin
34 Place on the schedule
35 Auto parts giant
36 Trick shot that knocks the balls off a French pool table?
38 Freely
39 Drew nigh
40 Old "public diplomacy" org.
42 Enthusiastic cheering section at a bullfight?
43 Unbroken
44 Just back from vacation, say
47 They do the thinking
50 River whose delta is Cape Tortosa
52 [sigh]
54 "Please?"
56 St. Andrews golf club member
60 Pacific kingdom
62 Like a cardinal
67 Promptly
68 Peace Nobelist called a "messenger to mankind"
70 Concerning
71 "Had enough?"
72 Lively tempo
73 Catkin bearers
74 Kind of blast
76 J. M. Barrie pirate
79 Flute, e.g.
81 Sweet after-dinner drinks

82 Additionally
83 "You've got to be kidding!"
85 Lend support to
86 ___ Coty, predecessor of Charles de Gaulle
89 Simple, pretty songs
93 Grandparents, often
95 No longer good
97 He hoped to succeed H.S.T.
101 Authorized to travel
102 Actress Anderson
104 Fishing gear with fine mesh wire
106 Garage job
109 Enzyme suffix
110 Simple headstone
111 Put on record, but not actually on a record
112 Intensifies, with "up"
114 Clarifying phrase
115 Rink leap
117 Sleek, for short
118 Jazzman Saunders
119 Tranquil scene
121 Suffix with front
123 Apology starter

by Fred Piscop

ACROSS

1 Carousel contents
5 Life may be spent here
11 Ones whose work isn't picking up
16 Flightless birds
21 Nabisco brand
22 Against
23 Country/rock singer Steve
24 "Anybody home?"
25 Start of a comment by 3- and 126-Down
28 Oil holder, maybe
29 Wig wearer
30 "It's __ to the finish"
31 Overhead bin, e.g.
33 Dearie
34 Kia model
36 Yellow or gray
37 Popped
38 1914 battle line
39 Comment, part 2
46 Brim
47 La-la lead-in
48 Trike rider
49 Some racehorses
50 Puffed up
54 Library Lovers Mo.
55 Natural pump outlet
57 Former U.N. chief U __
58 Comment, part 3
61 Proctor's call
63 Cabinet dept.
64 "So __ to offend . . ."
65 Phone book abbr.
66 Where many Sargents hang, with "the"
68 When repeated, an old TV sign-off
70 Spanish pronoun
71 Drink sometimes flavored with cinnamon
72 Whiz
74 Dirt in a dump truck, maybe
76 Isle of Mull neighbor
78 "The Torch in __" (Elias Canetti memoir)
79 & 81 Landmark 1972 album by 3- and 126-Down
83 Actress Van Devere
87 TV series featuring the war god Ares
89 D-Day transports: Abbr.
91 Very narrow, in a way
92 Football Hall-of-Famer Herber
93 Dated
96 Russian assembly
98 Spanish eyes
100 Damone of song
102 Land on Lake Chad
103 Swear
105 Lexicographer's study
107 Comment, part 4
110 Sloughs
112 Cape in the Holy See
114 Colorful moths
115 Piña __ (drinks)
116 Monetary unit of Panama
118 Where the Snake River snakes: Abbr.
119 Constellation near Cancer
120 Put out
121 Comment, part 5
125 Seventh-century year
129 Opera singer Mitchell of "Porgy and Bess"
130 Strand material
131 Afrique du __
132 Had in view
133 Most dear
136 Ken and Lena of Hollywood
138 Belt and hose, e.g.
141 "I'm __ here!"
142 End of the comment
145 Kind of call
146 Publication that clicks with readers?
147 Helping hands
148 A Sinatra
149 Some Romanovs
150 Honey bunch?
151 Entertain, as a child at bedtime
152 Real lulu

DOWN

1 Base for the old British East India Company
2 Indo-Europeans
3 With 126-Down, a noted humorist
4 Not so pleasant
5 Some hallucinogens, for short
6 Really clobber
7 Temporary
8 Recipe direction
9 Places for R.N.'s
10 Bubkes
11 Waste
12 Judge in 1990's news
13 Kill __ killed
14 R.&B. singer Cantrell
15 Establishes
16 Electrical resistor
17 Subject of many a sad ballad
18 Couturière Schiaparelli
19 Something to break or shake, in phrase
20 Unduplicated
26 Up to, in ads
27 Slangy commercial suffix
32 Activate, as a switch
35 String group, maybe
37 Put oneself where one shouldn't
39 "Beam __ . . ."
40 "__ no?"
41 Ride around
42 Order
43 "The Family Circus" cartoonist
44 Cousins of ospreys
45 Minute Maid Park player
46 Barely got along
50 One begins "The Lord is my light and my salvation"
51 Anthem start
52 Con game
53 Favoring bigger government, say
54 Kind of conservative
55 Bit of tomfoolery
56 With full force
59 Circus trainee
60 Butterfingers
62 Brian of early Roxy Music
67 Cinders of old comics
69 Straighten
73 Station along Route 66
75 Basis of a biblical miracle
77 Exuberant cry in Mexico
79 Now you see it, now you don't
80 NW Missouri city, informally
82 Cry one's head off
84 Opening for a coin?
85 Tuscany cathedral city
86 Ranch stock
88 Wrench's target
90 Sequel title starter
93 Latin dance
94 Feathered, say
95 Tulsa daily, with "the"
97 Show up
99 Trash pads?
101 Drink that's stirred
104 On-site supervisor?
106 Concocted
108 Night calls
109 What's expected
111 Midwest harvest
113 Noncellular phone
117 Wall St. figures
119 Lists
120 Led astray
122 Flexible reply
123 Plays peacemaker for
124 Bantu language
125 Not hearing
126 See 3-Down
127 Chant
128 Battle cry
132 Radar fig.
133 Toll
134 Baseball Hall-of-Famer Aparicio
135 Not this or that, in Spain
136 Medical suffix
137 Shoot up
139 Acerb
140 Italian bone
143 __ dye
144 Golfer Michelle

by Victor Fleming and Bonnie L. Gentry

ACROSS

1 See 131-Across
4 Root holders
10 End of "Lohengrin"
16 Minor player
19 Manning the quarterback
20 Good to go
21 Perfume bottle
22 Itinerary info: Abbr.
23 Yo-yo
24 Demonstration against a Miss America pageant?
26 Riddle-me-___
27 One making calls from home
29 Off one's feed
30 Tourist's aid
31 Fingerprint feature
33 Multiplying rapidly?
38 Legendary elephant eaters
40 Sinuous swimmer
41 It maddens MADD
42 Italian innkeeper
43 Loose rope fiber used as caulking
45 Ruckus
47 Shoebox letters
50 Grant-giving grp.
51 Collection of publications about historical advances?
58 Rush violently
59 Interstice
60 Northern Ireland politician Paisley and others
61 Dog it
63 Follower of Shakespeare?
65 Matter of aesthetics
66 Honored Fr. woman
67 Fab Four forename
68 One who accidentally blurts out "I did it!"?
75 De ___
76 Do-do connector
77 In excelsis ___
78 Perp prosecutors
79 ___ B'rith
80 Is indisposed
81 Use as a resource
82 Nobel-winning poet Heaney
87 Nose-picking and belching in the White House?
92 L.A.P.D. part
93 Work for eds.
94 Untilled tract
95 Coil inventor
96 Where people travel between poles?
100 "Little Birds" author
103 Twisted letter
105 Person who's not straight
106 Competitor's dedication to hard training?
111 Shaded spots
112 Carnation or rose
113 Gray spray
114 Come back again
117 Bird ___
118 Item to be checked on a census form?
123 Bit for an accelerator
124 Considerably
125 Taking prescription drugs, informally
126 Put something on
127 Ki ___ (Korea's legendary founder)
128 Antigua-to-Barbados dir.
129 What to see in a Chevrolet, in old ads
130 Got as a result
131 With 1-Across, an agreeable guy

DOWN

1 Course offerer
2 '06 class member, e.g.
3 Hairsplitter
4 One born on a kibbutz
5 "Splitting Heirs" actor
6 Patterned after
7 Tiger Stadium's sch.
8 Minor, at law
9 Like some hair
10 Recipient of much intl. aid
11 Opposite of tiptoe
12 Turkic language
13 Fruity frozen treat
14 Cyclades island
15 Unwelcome visitor
16 Healthful exercise, informally
17 Home of the John Day Fossil Beds National Monument
18 "The Quiet American" author
25 Bulldoze
28 Dig
32 4-Downs, e.g.
34 Really run
35 "Jenny" co-star, 1970
36 Feudal estate
37 Canines to beware of
38 "Zuckerman Unbound" novelist
39 Locale of Interstate H1
44 Teatro alla Scala locale
46 Players for prayers
48 Like some sees
49 Sister of Thalia
52 Contorted
53 Sometime sale site
54 Decided one would
55 Continuously
56 Male issue
57 Starchy foodstuff
62 In place of
64 With great strength
67 Take as an affront
68 Flyboys' hdqrs.
69 Pow!
70 Leave a mark on
71 Drain of color
72 Faith of fakirs
73 V.I.P. at V.P.I., say
74 Burkina ___
80 Stubborn sorts
83 Penguin variety
84 Nashville nickname
85 Where Lew Alcindor played
86 Critic's award
88 Touchy subject
89 Fails to be
90 Garlic relative
91 Whodunit title word
96 Gibes
97 Down Under denizens
98 Have covered
99 In
101 "___ robbed!"
102 More prone to pry
104 Flash light?
107 Pot-___ (French meat-and-vegetables dish)
108 Must have
109 Lyon is its capital
110 Under a spell
115 Watering aid
116 Some till fill
119 Abbr. after Sen. Judd Gregg's name
120 Nine-digit ID issuer
121 Org. that publishes American Hunter
122 Knock

by Mark Feldman

ACROSS

1 Pitch in
7 Sight near an igloo
11 Show utter disrespect to
17 Something in France
19 Plastic surgeon's target
22 *Discount brokerage formed in 1996
23 *Site of a famous drawing?
24 Scorch
25 My dear man
26 Run the show
28 Ratio phrase
29 Hardly raining?
32 *Writer who coined the word "booboisie"
35 Wane
38 Fee follower
39 Biological rings
40 Satellite counterpart
41 *Deceased writer whose work was the basis for a hit 2005 film
44 Kiss, in "Harry Potter"
45 Former Span. money
48 Something a bride may have
50 Newsman Potter and others
52 Doll
54 Old man of the sea, to Homer
55 Pop
57 How 265-pound football Hall-of-Famer Larry Little was named?
59 Legal hearing
60 Bonus
61 1939 Best Picture nominee banned in the Soviet Union
63 Year Chaucer died
65 *Kids' cookie makers, informally
68 Folk duo __ & Sylvia
69 Johnnycake
72 Porcelain piece
73 Alpine sight
76 Some takeout
77 Spy, at times
79 Damned doctor
82 First two words of "Waltzing Matilda"
83 Building contractor's study
84 These provide relief
85 __ Kosh B'Gosh
86 Language whose name means "army"
89 *1970's–80's TV villain
92 Knick rival
93 French West Indies isle, informally
95 Bit of a comic
96 Peter the Great's co-czar
98 *It was retired in 2005
101 Chestnut
103 Make __ for it
104 Capital of Belarus
107 As well
108 Daily __, "Spider-Man" newspaper
113 *QB who was the 1963 Player of the Year
116 *World order
119 Dumps
120 "Mission: Impossible" types
121 Skip
122 Seven __
123 Treat as a villain

DOWN

1 Its logo is four rings
2 Iced, with "up"
3 Waste
4 *Measure of brightness
5 Attorney's advice
6 Breviloquent
7 Peewee
8 Record producer __ Adler
9 Latin 101 verb
10 Regard
11 Barefoot
12 "Gotta catch 'em all!" sloganeer
13 Its logo is five rings: Abbr.
14 How Holmes beat Ali in '80
15 How chicken à la king may be served
16 Scandinavian language, to natives
17 Milk purchases: Abbr.
18 In the main
20 Fill up
21 University of North Carolina
27 Prot., for example
30 Some college staff
31 Tree that's a symbol of sorrow
33 "Don't Bring Me Down" grp., 1979
34 Pesters
35 Continental abbr.
36 *It provided tires for Lindbergh's Spirit of St. Louis
37 Good relations
39 "Just __!"
40 French Dadaist
42 Ones getting coll. counseling, maybe
43 Harry Bailly, in "The Canterbury Tales"
45 *Not for everyone
46 __ blue streak
47 Kind of race
49 Go with
51 Setting for part of Kerouac's "On the Road"
53 Kind of symbol
55 Precipitate
56 What Indiana once pursued
57 River to the Danube
58 "A seductive liar": George W. Ball
60 Grp. with balls and strikes
62 Ending with cash
63 Singer Marilyn
64 Film executive Harry and others
66 #26 of 26
67 Fall behind
70 Brussels-to-Amsterdam dir.
71 Nice ones
74 Neighbor of Rom.
75 Lab safety org.?
78 Hot and heavy, e.g.: Abbr.
79 Crosswords, say
80 The Runnin' Rebels, for short
81 Mach 1 passer
83 Like Larry of the Three Stooges, surprisingly
84 Healthy amount
87 Football positions: Abbr.
88 Pioneering German auto
90 __ boost
91 Barbara on the cover of 15 TV Guides
93 "Apollo 13" actor
94 Symbol of perfection
97 *Beetles
98 Lee of the old Milwaukee Braves
99 Look inside
100 Quiet, now
102 Truth, old-style
105 Figure (out)
106 Common arthroscopy site
109 Mountain West Conference team
110 Actress Gershon
111 1990's Senate majority leader
112 Nav. designation
114 Zenith
115 Singing syllable
117 Zenith rival
118 Chou En-__

by Derrick Niederman

ACROSS

1 Pop group with a hit Broadway musical
5 "Dido and Aeneas," for an early English example
10 Three-time Masters winner
15 Smack
19 Pasteleria offering
20 Had
21 Challenger's quest
22 Agitated, after "in"
23 Affectionate aquarium denizen?
25 Opposed to getting more angry?
27 Changes a mansard
28 Popular women's fragrance
30 Force in the Trojan War
31 French department
32 Glyceride, e.g.
33 Hatched
34 Monty Python member
37 Two-time L.P.G.A. Championship winner Laura
39 Grime fighter
40 Dark suit
42 Hub of a wheel
43 Grade enhancer
44 Does one's part
45 "Invasion of the Body Snatchers" invaders?
49 Trombonist Winding
52 Tiny amount
53 Preceder of Peter in a phonetic alphabet
54 Ear flap?
55 Listing
57 Less taxing
60 They're all that matter
62 A little flat?
63 At a slow pace
65 Evening thing
66 Sub
67 Wannabe surfers
68 Pluvial
69 Cot on wheels
70 "There's ___ for that"
71 Rhine feeder
72 Peach or beech
73 Panama, e.g.
76 "Miss Pym Disposes" author, 1946
77 Lettuce in the spring?
81 It's long in fashion
82 Actress Long and others
83 Beef cut
84 Discharged
86 Stink
90 It might raise a stink
92 ___-length
93 Ranchero wraps
94 Sine or cosine
95 Author of "Chaim Lederer's Return"
97 One offering compensation, maybe
98 Fit
99 Calm
102 Very scared insect?
104 Tainted tapioca?
107 Start of the Order of the Garter's motto
108 Bring down
109 Not done as well?
110 Switch attachment?
111 Puts on
112 Beat
113 Sty sound
114 Home, informally

DOWN

1 Patriots' grp.
2 Memory, sometimes
3 Invited
4 Sci-fi figures
5 Concert hall
6 Made pants?
7 Certain Prot.
8 Low-___
9 Stuff on tape
10 Union members
11 Number in C.B. lingo
12 Suffix with novel
13 Iran's Ayatollah ___ Khamenei
14 Actor William of "My Three Sons"
15 Desperado
16 Newscast segment
17 Sowing machine
18 Cremona product, for short
24 TV's Michaels
26 Stretch
29 Part of many a Civil War statue
32 Get out of
33 Blockhead
34 It's administered in H.S.
35 Capital whose Parliament house is called Fale Fono
36 The best time to elope?
38 Choice words
39 First or economy
41 Loot
43 Feather in one's cap
46 Hypnotist's directive
47 Deceiving
48 Old Nick
49 Young warmonger?
50 Others, in the Forum
51 Pour ___
56 Lyricist's need
58 Faithful servant in "As You Like It"
59 Lesser cut, usually
60 Not native
61 It fades in the fall
62 Play up
63 Pointer's reference
64 Primo
65 Oenone's husband, in myth
66 Like a defendant in court
68 Police car feature
69 Purplish
71 "So long"
72 Beat
74 Bit of skating practice
75 Marigraph activator
78 Take in too little
79 Rub the wrong way
80 Cubans' locations
81 Cousin of a herring
85 Went back and forth
86 Kind of acting
87 Near
88 Tour de France cyclist Floyd
89 Newspaper piece
90 Like Captain Kidd
91 Modern-day rhymer
93 Olympic skater Cohen
94 Awaken
96 End of many a race
98 Way up
99 ___-Asiatic
100 King
101 Hazzard County lawman
103 Category in baseball's Triple Crown: Abbr.
105 Athletic supporter
106 Caught on to

by Richard Silvestri

ACROSS

1 Not generic fashion
6 Hurry
11 Complaints
16 Soldier's fare, for short
19 Accustom
20 Appropriate
21 Full-length
22 Anthem contraction
23 Parent's admonishment
26 Records that are easily broken
27 Greets
28 Catchers
29 Drink with a three-leaf logo
31 Water source
32 26-Across, e.g.
35 Disorder
36 Landon of 1930's politics
39 1986 Pulitzer-winning novel set in a cattle drive
43 Computer-animated hit film of 1998
44 Vein holder
46 "In principio __ Verbum"
47 Hot, in Vegas
49 Delta hub
52 They're hooked
55 Satisfy
58 Paul Theroux novel made into a Harrison Ford film, with "The"
60 Hebrew name meaning "Hill of spring"
62 Biased
63 Solid South, once
65 Thus far
66 "__ my case"
69 Cheering loudly
71 Snap, e.g.
76 __-free
78 Dangerous place
84 Painting and printing, e.g.
86 1982 #1 hit with the lyric "living in perfect harmony"
89 Nixon commerce secretary Maurice
90 Dickens boy
92 Certain book addendum
93 Zip
95 Rossetti's "__ Ancilla Domini"
97 __ II, first man-made object to reach the moon
98 Baker's stock
100 Sign of affection
105 Form W-9 datum: Abbr.
106 Initial progress
108 Response to "am not"
109 Canon camera
111 Black ice, e.g.
112 About
114 Goes for the bells and whistles
119 Suffix with infant
120 TV announcer's exhortation
124 U.S.S.R. successor
125 Reds, once
126 Host of TV's "In Search Of . . ."
127 New Mexico county
128 Salon job
129 Candymaker Harry
130 Sends to Hades
131 Spring

DOWN

1 Gifts of greeting
2 One-two connector
3 Water mark?
4 Young's partner in accounting
5 Devastating
6 Un plus sept
7 Invite to one's home
8 Lyon who played Lolita
9 Word of encouragement
10 Gabriel Fahrenheit or Anders Celsius
11 Actor Young of the "Rocky" films
12 Specialist M.D.'s
13 Prefix with system
14 Causing more laughs
15 Strengthen
16 Soft rock?
17 Evangelist's cry
18 Imitation
24 Slimming procedure, briefly
25 One of two rivers forming the Ubangi
30 Personal, often
33 180-year-old in Genesis
34 Avoid
35 "Halt!"
36 Something to remember
37 Reveal
38 Two-timing
40 More trim
41 Adulterate
42 Minn. neighbor
45 Common Web site content
48 Olympics city after St. Moritz
50 Rapa __ (Easter Island)
51 More trim
53 Pat
54 Puerto Rico, e.g.
56 Paramedic's need
57 Seth and Abel's mother
59 Pablo Neruda's "__ to Common Things"
61 Online brokerage since 1993
64 __ Nostra
67 Curtain raiser?
68 Mug in a pub
70 Founder of the American Shakers
71 Duplicates, briefly
72 Bran material
73 Marmalade ingredient
74 Home of Carthage College
75 Superlative suffix
77 Little squirt
79 "Kid-tested, mother-approved" cereal
80 It can't be good
81 Part of a magical incantation
82 Smooths
83 Ronan __, "God Bless America" singer at Yankee Stadium
85 Didn't lie?
87 Flower girl, sometimes
88 Some pool sites
91 Bookkeeper's mailing: Abbr.
94 Through
96 Salad morsel
98 Law school class
99 One interested in net savings?
101 Grp. founded in Washington on 4/4/1949
102 Pulverized
103 Creator of Genesis
104 Somewhat
107 Where a person might get into a habit
110 "__ say . . ."
112 Bill producers
113 Site for sore eyes?
115 Sci. class
116 Lord in France
117 Net
118 Part of a piggy bank
121 Originally
122 Kind of operation
123 "Let me think about that . . ."

by Seth A. Abel

ACROSS

1 Thwacked but good
7 Come to one's senses
13 Trial case
20 Needing crackers, say
21 Spotted cat
22 More than tanned
23 Is acquainted with a quartet of wildebeests?
25 Consummate skill
26 Have coming
27 Poetic contraction
28 Religious sch.
30 Clears for liftoff
31 What is that in Mexico?
33 Community character
36 Drill one more time
38 Early run?
40 Booby-trapped nudist resort?
43 Soul buddy?
46 Skin ___
48 Cornmeal creation
49 Like 60% of people
51 Prudent time to get to the airport
54 ___ Dinh Diem of Vietnam
55 Old guy, slangily
56 Young guy, slangily
57 Subject of some gossip
61 Busy
62 Poet ___ García Lorca
65 Had plenty
66 "Once in Love With ___"
69 Vegetarians' supermarket protests?
73 "Um" cousins
74 Sulking more
76 One who's fallen
78 Home of the world's second-oldest written constitution, after America's
79 Make it big
82 Traveling
86 Old Olds models
87 Record producer Brian
88 Belief in disbelief
91 Contractions
92 Outskirts of the outskirts
96 Italian, e.g.
97 ___-wolf
98 Transported a couple of Porta-Potties?
101 C.S.I. evidence
102 Zoom in on
105 Sought morays
106 Foolish talk
108 "Fanny Hill," supposedly
110 Hockey's Tikkanen
112 Fifth and Mad.
114 Skip it
117 City on the Smoky Hill River
119 Rose raised by a sardonic gardener?
123 Less considered
124 Title heroine of a hit 2001 French film
125 Diplomat Harriman
126 Emotional
127 Busybodies
128 Towers above

DOWN

1 Expressway
2 Trollope's "Lady ___"
3 Place for strikes or strokes
4 Dots on a map
5 Salon workers, for short?
6 Nimble
7 Pointed
8 Main threat?
9 Calc. prerequisite
10 Blood sharers
11 Old French coins
12 Results of piercing pain?
13 1972 treaty subj.
14 Available on the stock exchange
15 "And they went ___ in a Sieve": Edward Lear
16 Robin Williams-esque
17 Eastern European guy who loves both sexes?
18 Word turned into its own opposite by putting a T in front
19 Big name in ice cream
24 Shy person?
29 Candy billed as "The Freshmaker"
32 Heed
34 She was famously married 3/20/69 at the Rock of Gibraltar
35 Initials for two Belushis
37 Bagged leaves
38 Horizontal, perhaps
39 Oktoberfest serving
41 "Exodus" hero
42 Word on a wall, in the Bible
44 Vulture, e.g.
45 Beginnings
47 Symbol on the front of some bars
49 Halt
50 Mideast capital
52 Campaign dirty trick
53 Trumpeter on the "Kill Bill" soundtrack
55 "___ go!"
58 Sis, e.g.
59 Horned Frogs' sch.
60 Kind of pain
63 Key of "The James Bond Theme"
64 List for St. Peter
65 Fidgety
66 Horrifies
67 Cabbage
68 Christmas quilters' haze?
70 Number cruncher, for short
71 Ad follow-up?
72 "Wait ___!"
75 Poi source
77 Individually
79 One-spot
80 En route
81 Oval-shaped loaf
83 Alternative energy source
84 Speller's phrase
85 Community ctr.
89 Prefix with realist
90 Teeny, slangily
92 Manhattan, for one: Abbr.
93 Follower of Manhattan
94 Milk source
95 Convalescent sites
98 Noble partner
99 Current resisters
100 Had too much
103 "The Prince of Tides" co-star
104 Certain 60's protest
107 Bouquet
108 When repeated, a dolphinfish
109 Abba of Israel
111 French weapon
113 Calif. force
115 Ill-gotten gains
116 Mound stats
118 Poetic preposition
120 Long
121 Place for a toothpick
122 Postgrad field

by Lee Glickstein and Ben Tausig

ACROSS

1 Major-league team with the most season losses, 120, in the 20th century
5 Fills positions for
11 A mouse moves over it
14 "Get ___!"
17 Former enemy capital
18 Kind of wrestling
19 House painting attire, maybe
22 Electrolysis particle
23 Whining from execs?
25 Be slightly turned on?
27 "Son of Frankenstein" role
28 Mint family plant
29 Rock guitarist Barrett
30 Flight
32 Pens and needles
35 "Summer of Sam" director
36 Day ___
39 Laid up
41 "Yikes!"
42 Fashionable gun?
47 Lose resilience
49 Ringside shout
50 Regard
52 Cheesy snack
53 Engineering project begun in 1898
55 Usher to, as a table
57 Princess of Power
58 Money in the bag, maybe
59 "Well, this pays the rent"
61 Bug
62 Whit
63 Deletes
66 "Then join you with them, like ___ of steel": Shak.
67 Assistants at a Kate Spade factory?
71 Valle del Bove locale
72 ___ Park, N.J.
74 NASA vehicle
75 Part of a winning combination
76 Irish-born actress McKenna
78 Washer setting
80 Like James Brown's music
82 Snoops
83 Someone sexy
85 60 shares, e.g.
87 Cordial
88 The Wildcats of the N.C.A.A.
89 New England hockey hero
90 Unit amount of sunlight seen?
92 Knotted up
94 Central
96 Suffix with Ecuador
97 Accident
100 Missouri city, briefly
102 Flit (about)
103 Equi- equivalent
106 Motivated
109 As recently as
111 Reunion no-shows?
115 Hemlock?
118 Go blading
119 Literary orphan
120 Swimming
121 Glacial ice formation
122 Three of a kind, in poker parlance
123 Suffix with bass
124 Scenic vistas, briefly
125 African antelope

DOWN

1 Stick
2 Isolate
3 Play garden produce like a horn?
4 New York's Mount ___ Hospital
5 No-no's opposite?
6 Letter-shaped fastener
7 Mine entrances
8 In a proper manner
9 Braved
10 High-hatter
11 Beer can feature
12 ___ right
13 W.W. II event
14 Shaggy sponsor of a sort?
15 Lodge
16 N.Y.C. arena
17 "The Laughing Cavalier" artist
20 Sprightly dances
21 Brief online message
24 A. A. for children
26 Place trailers are in
31 Wires
33 ___ land
34 Footnote word
37 Grenade part
38 Santa ___ (hot winds)
39 To whom "We'll always have Paris" was spoken
40 Time for crowing
43 Key with three sharps: Abbr.
44 Separation
45 "Voilà!"
46 Examination of an English royal house?
48 Phazyme alternative
50 Raison ___
51 Relieving knee pain?
53 Uninteresting
54 Cat's sniffer?
55 Kingdom of Broadway
56 Beat
60 Long jumper
62 Inconstant
64 Prevent from making a hit?
65 Gets some color
68 Wreck site
69 Supermarket chain
70 Nurse
73 Able to see right through
77 "Say as he says, ___ shall never go": "The Taming of the Shrew"
79 Gang land
80 Farm young
81 Old
83 "Gilligan's Island" dwellings
84 Attending to a task
86 F.D.R. plan
90 They meet in the middle
91 ___-European
93 "Go, and catch a falling star" poet
95 City connected to Philadelphia by the Benjamin Franklin Bridge
98 Where kites may be found
99 Canon competitor
101 Sommer in the cinema
103 Ishmael's half-brother
104 Rap relative
105 Ready to be drawn
107 "One Good Cop" actress
108 Tiny time period: Abbr.
110 Jerk
112 ID's with two hyphens
113 It may be given from father to son
114 PC screens
115 Station personalities
116 Actress ___ Dawn Chong
117 Back again

by Joe DiPietro

MISSING PERSONS

ACROSS

1 Outstanding football player
7 Keep after further changes
13 Indian-related
19 Letter-shaped tesserae
20 Little sucker
21 He wrote "Even the worthy Homer sometimes nods"
22 Store I most like to shop at?
24 Ready for publication
25 Comic Auerbach
26 2600, 5200 and 7800, gamewise
27 Photo ___
29 Site of July 1944 fighting
30 Jack who hosted the 1950's game show "Dotto"
32 Mouse catcher, in Madrid
34 Actress Aniston, to friends
36 Missing from 22-Across
37 Melee in a Dumpster?
42 Fix up, as old floors
45 "Too bad"
46 1957 hit for the Bobbettes
47 Combine
48 Hang around
51 Missing from 119-Across
52 ___ Corner, Va. (Washington suburb)
53 N.R.C. forerunner
54 What you will
55 Cabbie's call
57 Worked (up)
58 Missing from 73-Down
59 Clothing retailer beginning in 1969
60 Flipper?
62 Most calm
65 Discounted by
66 Rouses
68 Seasonal beverage
69 Perennial best-seller subjects
71 Medieval chest
74 Dr. Egon ___ ("Ghostbusters" role)
77 Imagine
81 Signals
83 Missing from 13-Down
84 Busy travel day, typically
86 East German secret police
87 Baseball Hall-of-Famer Al
88 Actress Gardner
89 Glacial ridges
91 Missing from 61-Down
92 Where Zaragoza is
93 Blue Stater, more likely than not
94 Pioneering weather satellite
95 Federico of Clinton's cabinet
96 Novel
98 Place to wash clothes in old Rome?
100 U.S. News or YM
102 Gold units: Abbr.
103 Vater's boy
105 Memorable 1966 hurricane
106 "I Ain't Marching Anymore" singer
108 Cry of surprise
110 Overflowed
113 Arab capital
117 Senator's locale
119 Droid in an oil container?
122 Looked like Groucho
123 Some T-shirt designs
124 Arose
125 Pitcher's quote
126 Cops' weapons
127 Tone deafness

DOWN

1 Soprano Gluck
2 Astronomical meas.
3 Good news on a gloomy day, e.g.
4 Objections
5 Exhibit
6 Baja bruin
7 Missing from 37-Across
8 Forces
9 Apelike
10 Starbuck's order?
11 Dictionary abbr.
12 Prefix with -derm
13 A particular bit of typography?
14 Casting need
15 It's usually blue, green or brown
16 Certain eligibility requirement for Little League?
17 Amtrak service
18 Deceived
20 Where Kofi Annan received an M.B.A.
23 Finely honed
28 Attire with pics of sheep, maybe
31 ___ Martin (cognac)
33 Source of spices for old traders
35 Charlie Chan player on TV
37 Soaks
38 Thrown for ___
39 Super Bowl XXXVII winner, for short
40 Sheet of ice
41 Leanings
43 Go over
44 Communications orbiter
47 Get by
49 Pilots' info
50 Sales crew
52 Bolt holder
56 "Maybe this is fate"
58 "Be ___" ("Help me out")
61 Heeds humorist George?
63 Memory trace
64 Across
67 Jon with the 1992 hit "Just Another Day"
70 "___ of the D'Urbervilles"
71 "Lonely Boy" singer
72 Crowd sound
73 What you hear on a Chris Rock recording?
75 Faux "buttons"
76 Hoist again, as a sail
78 Whiz
79 Not abstaining
80 Type measures
82 Actress Aimée
85 Missing from 16-Down
89 Expiate
90 Airer of many games
95 Founder of Lima
97 Show to a seat, informally
98 1992 Elton John hit
99 Postgame productions
100 Cabbage
101 Functioned
104 Four Holy Roman emperors
107 Missing from 98-Across
109 Passing mention?
111 Range: Abbr.
112 Quizzical sounds
114 OPEC member
115 Italian artist Guido
116 Saint from Kiev
118 Dripping
120 Mouths, zoologically
121 Org. receiving royalties for "God Bless America"

by Brendan Emmett Quigley

ACROSS

1 With 126-Across, author of the quip starting at 27-Across
6 Kind of race
10 "Come Back, Little Sheba" playwright
14 Modern home of the 10-Down
18 Product sold with a bag
20 "Hop ___!"
21 Tyros
23 Bill Clinton memoir
24 Nasty sort
25 Effecting a release
26 Blue
27 Start of a quip from Court and Society Review, 1887
30 V.I.P.
32 Literature Nobelist Morrison
33 What "Lucy in the Sky With Diamonds" may or may not be about
34 Quip, part 2
38 Edit
44 "An Affair to Remember" star, 1957
45 Berlioz's "Les nuits d'___"
46 Man of mystery
47 Layered
48 Project completion?
49 King Minos, for one
52 Site for Franklin Roosevelt
54 Matter of debate
55 Pageant prize
57 Quip, part 3
60 "It's about time!"
62 Lucre
63 Energizer or Duracell option
64 Low-value wad
65 Quip, part 4
70 "The Thief of Bagdad" actor, 1940
73 Ramallah grp.
74 Mystique
75 W.W. II wolf pack
79 Quip, part 5
83 "Rubber Duckie" singer of children's TV
84 See 112-Down
85 Winter pear
86 Brynhild's beloved
90 Granting grp.
91 It can be found in a tree
93 Cry with eyes lit up
95 4×4
96 Cold war winner
97 Huge, to Hugo
98 Quip, part 6
102 Lao-___
104 Dutch export
105 Dia's opposite
106 End of the quip
113 Try to win, in a way
116 Like a Swiss Army knife
117 One of a sailing trio
118 Time competitor, informally
120 Used a crowbar on, maybe
121 Election day: Abbr.
122 Fish that may someday spawn
123 Call after a hammer is hit
124 Agrippina's slayer
125 Prize since 1949
126 See 1-Across

DOWN

1 ___ law
2 Nutritious bean
3 Breakfast in a box
4 Flying start?
5 Common ink purchase
6 Tittle
7 It's read word for word
8 Fun house item
9 "Revolution From Within" author
10 Old inhabitant of 14-Across
11 With every hair in place
12 Ones dressed in black
13 F.D.A.-banned supplement
14 Match player?
15 Dramatic rebuke
16 Scout leader?
17 S O S responder: Abbr.
19 Satisfied subscriber, apparently
22 Part of a manger scene
28 Stem
29 Poet with the longtime NPR program "A Word in Your Ear"
31 Pencil holder, sometimes
34 Muscular watchdog
35 Sparked anew
36 "But on the other hand . . ."
37 Early sixth-century year
39 Put out
40 Stain
41 Actor Williams of "Happy Days"
42 Revolution, for one
43 Hammock supports
47 Sic on
49 Bills, e.g.
50 Exactly, after "to"
51 Court plea, briefly
53 Anne of comedy
56 Bygone Crayola color
58 Black piano key
59 Pearl City setting
61 Imbibe
62 Brigham Young University site
66 "Let's ___ There" (1980's NBC slogan)
67 Dim responses
68 ". . . ___ saw Elba"
69 Retired
70 Tired
71 Mark Twain/Bret Harte play
72 Game of chance
76 "Black Beauty" author
77 Link with
78 ___ Tranquillity
80 Offer that seems too good to be true, probably
81 Birthright seller
82 Lug
87 Floor (it)
88 Knoxville sch.
89 Get back on track
92 Begin something, in slang
94 Just firm enough
96 Lofty degree
98 It's a test
99 Element that quickly oxidizes in air
100 Artist with the 2002 #1 hit "Lose Yourself"
101 Winter fishing tool
103 Not attack head-on
106 Family viewing mark
107 "My ___!"
108 March slogan word
109 Dawning response
110 "Way cool!"
111 Strange: Prefix
112 With 84-Across, very simple
114 Had to settle
115 Bone head?
119 Application form abbr.

by Mark Diehl and Kevin McCann

ACROSS

1 Mitsubishi S.U.V.
8 Knocked their socks off
15 Earth
20 Wake-up call, e.g.
21 It may be said after kissing the tips of one's fingers
22 Healing plants
23 What the peddler owes?
25 B-ball
26 Bust ___
27 Construction material in King Solomon's temple
28 National rival
30 Driver's aid
31 Maker of the first walkie-talkie
34 "All My ___ Live in Texas" (1987 #1 country hit)
36 Berate
38 Lt.'s subordinate
39 Top Tatar's tattler?
44 Jellied dishes in England
45 Place for a father-to-be: Abbr.
46 First name in gossip
47 Passes
49 Squad leaders: Abbr.
52 Way to the top
54 Shirt tag info
56 Not knowing what to do
59 "You're ___!" (Archie Bunker comment)
60 Advice for an understaffed yachtsman?
63 ___ seul (solo dance)
64 Change for a fin
66 Net alternative
67 Close pitches
69 Kind of acid
70 Unable to get loose
74 Site of a 1797 Napoleon victory
75 Cause of some spots
77 Screwball
78 Apple holder, maybe
80 St. Martin, e.g.
81 Result of whipping?
85 Architect William Van ___
86 Simmons competitor
88 Suffix with flex
89 Cartoonist who drew the Shmoo
90 Mimics
91 Some hotel visits
93 Summer coolers
95 Clamor
96 Spanish for "are"
98 Best-selling baseball equipment?
102 Sec
105 Neverland
107 Common street name
108 At no charge
110 Classic New Yorker cartoonist ___ Irvin
111 100 centimes
114 ___ set (group of tools)
117 Early Beatles, affectionately
118 "The Goat, or Who is Sylvia?" writer
120 Packer fan's angry cry after an interception?
124 Massey of "Rosalie"
125 Slimmest election margin
126 Cupidity
127 Cake part
128 Balcony's edge
129 Gifts

DOWN

1 ___ Defarge of "A Tale of Two Cities"
2 Hells Canyon locale
3 "Quit your excuses"
4 All, in music
5 That, to Tadeo
6 Call
7 Ouija, e.g.
8 Blue dye
9 Dancing girl in "The Return of the Jedi"
10 "The ground ___ she trod", Milton
11 Urban carriers
12 Patterned fabric
13 Operation Exodus participant
14 "Every ___ king"
15 Literally, "big water"
16 Grp. with the 1977 platinum album "Out of the Blue"
17 Hoboes by nature?
18 Anti-Prohibitionist's cause
19 Ledger column
24 Burn
29 Repetitive sort
32 Delivery lines: Abbr.
33 Law man?
35 Unknown
37 Riga native
40 Show horse
41 Ring figure
42 Ox-eyed queen of myth
43 Means to ___
45 Fla. vacation spot
48 Black currant flavor in wines
49 Bush activities
50 Skeletal support in a sponge
51 Muppet seller's gender guideline?
52 Lao-___
53 1940's first lady
55 Woeful words
57 Flashback caption
58 Transfers
60 Cry made with one's arm behind one's back
61 Less than right?
62 Real-life boxing champ who appeared in "Rocky II"
65 Lubrication channel
68 VCR insert
71 Bottom-of-letter abbr.
72 Panpharmacon
73 Insomnia cause
76 O'Connor successor
79 Alley ___
82 Recipe abbr.
83 Fast server?
84 Island that's part of 90-Down: Abbr.
87 Big fat mouth
90 See 84-Down: Abbr.
92 Clash (with)
94 Floor wiper
95 Elevs.
96 Overseas train service
97 ___ Artois, beer from Belgium
99 "Mr. Belvedere" co-star
100 Hit man
101 Pawed
102 Attract
103 Blue-pencil
104 Impatient agreement
106 Start to a bit of bad news
109 Blaze
112 Opposite of under
113 Kid watcher
115 Suffix with electro-
116 Sarcastic comment
119 Little Rock-to-Memphis dir.
121 Seductive Longoria
122 New Deal inits.
123 Chess champion Mikhail

by Ashish Vengsarkar

ACROSS

1 Slanted
7 Silly smile
13 "Le Rhinocéros" playwright
20 Protracted prayer
21 Relative of a rhododendron
22 Start of a hole
23 Job for a ballroom dance instructor?
25 Refuse to help in the garden?
26 Is in the Vatican
27 Sing ___ Daily, major Hong Kong newspaper
28 Altar in the sky
29 "Nonsense!"
31 Internet message
32 Discovery accompaniers
34 Job for a lingerie salesclerk?
38 Popeye, for one
39 Divine
41 Jimjams
42 Sainted pope called "the Great"
43 No. of People, say
44 Start of Idaho's motto
45 Anatomical enclosure
47 Banks on
50 Vegetable with sushi
52 Officer who may not be in uniform
55 Elects
56 Bus. runners
59 Job for a coffee shop employee?
64 Base approval
66 Shrinks' org.
67 Modern music genre
68 Blocks
70 Mucho
71 Mass. summer setting
72 "Family ___"
74 Decorate, as a 54-Down
75 It rolls on a Rolls
77 127-Down grp.
78 PC user's shortcut
80 Fearsome weapon
83 Martinmas's mo.
84 Grind
85 Miscellany
87 Job for a high school teacher?
90 Diamond of note
91 Bite
93 Suffix with super
94 Info at SFO
95 "Forget it"
98 Sermon subject
100 Man chaser?
103 Fix
105 "___ take arms . . ."
106 Queen of the fairies
109 Rosencrantz or Guildenstern, in "Hamlet"
112 Least bit
113 Job for an architect?
116 Roughly
117 Yawning
119 What a keeper may keep
120 Poetic ending with how
121 Idled
123 The Divine, to da Vinci
124 "With All Disrespect" essayist
126 Job for a business tycoon?
130 Supremely spooky
131 Skirts
132 Putter's near-miss
133 Jilts
134 Mixture of many spices, in Indian cookery
135 Ties a no-frills knot?

DOWN

1 Green
2 It has a tip for a ballerina
3 Rama and Krishna, e.g.
4 Was up
5 Quick approval: Abbr.
6 Appetite whetter
7 Baseball's Maglie
8 "The Compleat Angler" author Walton
9 Siege site of 1936–39
10 Flexible
11 Extra-wide spec
12 Farriers' tools
13 Most eager to go
14 Antipoverty agcy.
15 Moriarty, to Holmes
16 X Games airer
17 Job for a film photographer?
18 Multi-Emmy-winning NBC sportscaster
19 Bewhiskered animals
24 Subject heading for strategizers
30 In a tizzy
33 Party prep
35 Worrisome mechanical sound
36 Prime meridian std.
37 Kids' jumping game
40 Absolutely fabulous
46 Italian sweetheart
48 Farm measures
49 "___ Excited" (Pointer Sisters hit)
51 "This one's ___"
53 More cordlike
54 See 74-Across
57 Flub
58 Development sites
59 Subordinate deity, in classical myth
60 Modernize
61 Job for a dating service counselor?
62 Ascend
63 "You can't get out this way"
65 Lift
69 Harmony
73 Where some major arteries go
76 Medea, for one
79 Move, in Realtor-speak
81 Box
82 Certain specialty docs
86 See 108-Down
88 Competitor of State Farm
89 Handled
92 Disgraces
96 Hobbyist with toy trains, e.g.
97 J.F.K. debater in 1960
99 Chinese restaurant sign
101 Help from on high
102 What's left
103 Steamy, maybe
104 "Hear, hear!"
107 Early NASA rockets
108 With 86-Down, popular serial comic strip beginning in 1940
110 Functional
111 Settles down for the night
114 Against a thing, legally
115 Cantilevered window
118 Dancer's dip
122 It might make you a sweater
125 Suffix with spiritual
127 The Cavaliers of coll. football
128 Hush-hush grp.
129 Mil. mail depot

by Norma Johnson & Nancy Salomon

ACROSS

1 How sale goods may be sold
8 Hardy bulbs
13 Hockey game starter, often
20 Contract
21 Even if, briefly
22 Humbled
23 Ann Landers, e.g.
24 Further shorten, maybe
25 Fooled around
26 Dirty coat
27 Hollywood stars, e.g.
29 Hang loose
31 Swim routine
32 Chaps
33 Henna and others
34 Helgenberger of "C.S.I."
38 Heroine of a Gershwin opera
39 Horse course
41 Swing around
45 Praise from a choir
47 "Here ___."
49 "Holy mackerel!" and others
50 -
52 Utilizes fully
53 -
55 Where to find an eBay listing
56 It's often left hanging
57 ___ Brazzi, star of "South Pacific"
58 Harvester ___
59 Personae non ___
62 Cur
63 Conforming to
67 Sympathetic
68 -
69 Hands down
70 Williams with a crown, once
77 Hits hard
78 Mr. Big, e.g.
79 High points
80 Suffix with Ecuador
81 Bilingual Muppet
84 Legendary
85 -
89 Soldier's accessory of old
90 -
91 Actress Gardner
92 Precisely
93 Hymn pronoun
94 Small racer
96 Honks off, so to speak
98 B. D. ___ of Broadway's "M. Butterfly"
99 Staff note
101 Henley who wrote "Crimes of the Heart"
102 Hopper
106 Irish revolutionary Robert
107 Had dinner at home
109 Natty sorts
113 Vulnerable to fire
115 Product label abbr.
117 Teases
119 Kind of family
120 Masonry, for one
121 Shows
122 Hands out, as homework
123 Some HDTV's
124 Haifa money

DOWN

1 Hieroglyphic figures
2 Huxtable boy, on "The Cosby Show"
3 Florence is on it
4 Trap contents
5 Some ducts carry them
6 Highway behemoth
7 Heavy hitters
8 "Haven't Got Time for the Pain" singer, 1974
9 Like non-oyster months
10 Some score notations, for short
11 Leafy green
12 "Thanks, pal"
13 Ancient
14 Soft-soap
15 Leather sticker
16 Carter of sitcomdom
17 Part of a score
18 Heavy
19 Interjects
28 Heave-hos
30 Go after, as a rebound
34 Hepburn, Garbo and Gable employer, once
35 Huntsville's home: Abbr.
36 Seoul soldier
37 Rocky Mountains line
38 Tip of Manhattan
40 Very expensive contest prizes?
41 Hera, to Persephone
42 Drug once available under the commercial name Delysid
43 Emma player in "The Avengers"
44 Fancy name appendage
46 Hebrew of old
48 Diamond cutter?
49 Series terminal
51 Macho way to fight
54 Old atlas abbr.
59 Former high-tech co.
60 "Citizen X" star, 1995
61 Response: Abbr.
64 Cousin ___ of "The Addams Family"
65 Name separator
66 Dept. store stuff
70 Ad ___ (how tariffs may be assessed)
71 Homes, for some
72 Norse goddess of fate
73 Heckler's missile
74 "I ___ bad moon rising"
75 Hand cleaners at the dinner table
76 Phoenician fertility deity
81 Bit of sch. writing
82 "How exciting!"
83 Halmstad's locale: Abbr.
86 "How was ___ know?"
87 Place for a duck
88 Hosp. readout
95 -
97 -
100 County with the White Sands National Monument
101 Blue
102 Howe who wrote "Pride's Crossing"
103 Weight
104 Hyperbola parts
105 "Hallucinogenic Toreador" artist
106 New York cardinal
108 First name in a dictionary
109 Hall-of-Fame catcher Carlton
110 Plains native
111 Apostle who wrote "Ye see how large a letter I have written"
112 Heathrow sights, once
114 Photog's image
116 Spank
118 Heavy-duty cleanser

by Harvey Estes

ACROSS

1 Modern wall hanging
5 Military letters
9 Kind of case in grammar: Abbr.
12 Fruit of a flower
19 Place
20 Water carrier
21 Shetland turndown
22 Nail polish remover
23 Cheery fellow in the neighborhood?
26 One for the books
27 "You got that right!"
28 Slowly ascended
30 Class clown, e.g.
31 More furtive
32 Actress Kelly
33 Empties (of)
35 Bit of tax planning, for short
36 Excellent portrayal of a Gary Cooper role?
39 Hitch
40 Brainy
45 Work periods
46 Fireplace
47 Social breakdown
48 Turkish title
49 Answer men
50 "Let me repeat . . ."
51 Tattoo an anonymous source?
56 Dried coconut meat
57 Charlotte ___
58 "Holy mackerel!"
59 Night spot
60 Clears
61 Something to "call me" per an old song . . . or a hint to this puzzle's theme
65 Tin Man's malady
68 Let up
70 Turn red or yellow, say
71 Impermissible
72 Flat storage site
73 "The A-Team" actor on the cover of GQ?
76 Lines on a staff
77 Presenter of a likeness?
78 Start of a Latin conjugation
79 Minnesota college
80 Match
81 "Enough!"
84 Gemstone quality
86 Running in circles?
87 Father's song about a 79-Down character?
89 Bard's "before"
90 Pull (in)
91 "It's Too Late Now" autobiographer
92 All in ___ work
97 Mountain climber, e.g.
99 Saint whose feast day is December 25
102 1969 hit by the Who
103 Nuts
105 Get a bald advertising icon out of the slammer?
107 In pieces
108 Father figures
109 Cover girl Heidi
110 Razor name
111 AOL alternative
112 Sheffield-to-London dir.
113 Big name in games
114 Outdoor wedding rental

DOWN

1 Returnees from Mecca
2 Not laugh-out-loud funny, perhaps
3 Place for a programme
4 Dance in France
5 "This is right ___ alley"
6 Mediterranean isl.
7 Keep from overheating, in a way
8 Rococo
9 Recipe amount
10 Starr of the N.F.L.
11 Bach's "___, Joy of Man's Desiring"
12 Campus figs.
13 Candles in a menorah, e.g.
14 They may go under the arms
15 Response to a backstabber
16 Putting up a guy in the bath?
17 Among other things
18 Aristocracies
24 "Babi ___" (Yevtushenko poem)
25 They may make you sick
29 Kind of income
32 Extinct flightless bird
34 Security needs
36 Test before further studies, for short
37 Geom. line
38 Many a NASA employee: Abbr.
39 Showy bloom
40 Stone heap
41 Come after
42 Honored a monocled man at the Friars Club?
43 Diplomats
44 Wait
46 Game player's gleeful cry
49 View by computed tomography
51 Noted polar explorer
52 Charles, for one
53 Natural bristles
54 Wyo. neighbor
55 John on a farm
59 Angled
61 Attention-getting cry
62 Open . . .
63 Typing test stat.
64 Election closer?
66 RC's, e.g.
67 Fashion plates, in British lingo
69 Low part of a high top
71 Place for a béret
72 Havana's home
73 Column material
74 "Typee" sequel
75 Idiotic
77 Pitcher
79 See 87-Across: Abbr.
81 Turn red or yellow, say
82 Dunk
83 Singer Lopez
84 Achieve through trickery
85 ___ St.-Louis, Paris
87 Mabel who sang "Fly Me to the Moon"
88 Lighthouse signals
90 Aptly named author Charles
92 Film buff's channel
93 Key of Prokofiev's Piano Concerto No. 1
94 Mountain ridge
95 Pine
96 Overseas assembly
98 Mozart's ___ Symphony (No. 36)
100 Mail letters
101 College application nos.
102 "Joy of Cooking" author Rombauer
104 Sign of success
106 Kisser

by Elizabeth C. Gorski

ACROSS

1 Fooling (around)
8 Open, in a way
13 7, on modern phones
17 Alternatively
21 "Way to go!"
22 Weeping daughter of Tantalus
23 Perfectly, after "to"
24 Must have
25 White ___ House
27 Moved to and fro
29 Adds to the pot, say
30 Each
31 "The Sound of Music" name
33 Hunting canine
34 Intermittently, after "off"
35 Small spray
37 Muse of mimicry
39 Singer Mann
40 Big name in faucets
41 N.L. East team, on scoreboards
42 Double ___ play
45 Sun. talks
46 Loop loopers
47 Streamlined
49 Some E.M.S. cases
50 Address
52 U.S. 1, for one: Abbr.
53 Ultrapatriot
55 Ole Miss rival
56 Postgrad degs.
59 Orange ___ Bowl
66 Sign of love . . . or rejection
68 Heavenly hunter
69 Bruin
70 One given "unto us," in Isaiah
71 Sundae topper
72 Spur (on)
73 Defeater of R.M.N.
74 Latin twinklers
75 Monocle part
76 Easter ___ bunny
85 Airline rarity, increasingly
86 Had a lame-duck session, say
87 Part missing from a vest
88 Poet laureate before Southey
89 Fails to
91 Attending to the matter
92 Too, in Toulouse
95 Skater Slutskaya
97 Had
98 e ___ Bay
101 Comprehend
102 Answer to the riddle "The higher it goes, the less you hear it"
104 Stand
105 Early third-century year
106 Alternatives
108 Engine part
109 Nada
111 F.B.I. facility
114 Thickening agent
117 New ___ Latin
120 Head's opposite
121 Only: Fr.
122 Fanatical
124 Fab Four name
125 Whacks
127 Part of MGM
128 Tropical fruits
130 Like many benefit tournaments
132 Computer file suffix
133 University in Greenville, S.C.
134 Like the 1915 San Francisco Mint $50 gold coin
136 Flag ___ Day
139 Exhausted
140 Seconds
141 Words after "put an" or "see no"
142 Fit for consumption
143 Time long past
144 Cornerstone abbr.
145 "The Exorcist" actor, with "von"
146 :-) :-) :-)

DOWN

1 It's tied up in knots
2 Tractor powerer, maybe
3 Progress
4 Printemps, par exemple
5 Norwegian playwright
6 Relatives of AND's and OR's in Boolean logic
7 High school class
8 Big name in auto racing
9 Kind of acid
10 Where streets meet: Abbr.
11 Support
12 Noblewoman
13 Contents of some patches
14 i ___ Pod
15 Gas station abbr.
16 Darns
17 Body ___ language
18 Lentil or bean
19 Petitioner
20 Whirlpools
26 Big ___ time
28 Bond rating
32 MGM motto opener
35 Start of many Québec place names
36 Former Patriots QB Steve
38 Mountain nymph
41 Pub offerings
43 Something carbon monoxide lacks
44 Rep.'s opposite
47 Render speechless
48 German canal name
51 Nut in mixed nuts
52 Varig destination
54 Hush-hush govt. org.
56 Abdominal pouches
57 Down's opposite: Abbr.
58 Blue shade
59 Average guys
60 Spur (on)
61 Bone connector
62 Take into custody
63 Beauty queen's wear
64 "The Thin Man" pooch
65 Actress Martin, star of TV's "National Velvet"
67 Tape, say
71 Dollar, slangily
73 Shock
74 It's the law
77 Suffix with Congo
78 Bit of beachwear
79 Setting for part of "King Henry VI, Part 2"
80 Mideast bigwig
81 Himalayan sighting
82 Hindu titles
83 Harmony
84 Furniture wood
89 Follow relentlessly
90 Show a deficit
92 Reproducing without fertilization
93 Letters at sea
94 1956 trouble spot
95 Desire
96 Goal for a D.H.
98 Trivial Pursuit edition
99 Kind of tide
100 Latin "behold!"
103 Former CBS military show
106 Buck ___ eye
107 In a tangle
108 Chianti containers
110 Part of L.A.
111 "Go away!"
112 With respect to hearing
113 Lightheaded people?
114 Fleet of ships
115 Bola user
116 One who suspends an action, at law
118 Leandro's love, in a Mancinelli opera
119 Urban renewal target
121 Soap format
123 Hammarskjöld of the U.N.
126 U-shaped river bend
127 Civvies
129 A portion
131 When repeated, a top five hit of 1968 or 1987
133 Deception
135 Turndowns
137 Like 9 or 5
138 Former defense secretary Aspin

by Derrick Niederman

ACROSS

1 Big rays
7 A little dirty
11 Fly nets?
15 Deer hunter
19 Golden Crinkles maker
20 Product in a tub
21 Mosque overseer
22 A part of
23 Bare
24 In a ___, there's at least one fluid ounce of ___
27 In a ___, there's a volume of ___ that keeps it firm
29 Designer Alvar
30 Symbol of Ireland
31 "Sixteen Tons" singer's workplace
32 In a ___, there's plenty of sweet ___ to be harvested
36 Nonexistent
37 Come by
39 Root used in perfumery
40 In a ___, you can periodically catch a ___
46 Entry need, maybe
48 Part of FWIW
49 Stackable snackables
50 Burst of energy
51 See 5-Down
52 Pounding
53 In ___, you might see some ___ hanging around
55 The America's Cup trophy, e.g.
56 Trueheart of "Dick Tracy"
57 "Foucault's Pendulum" author
58 Kind of bran
59 Region holding ancient Ephesus
62 Nuptial agreement
64 Scattered
66 In a ___, there's no shortage of ___ to drink
68 Targets
72 Red, white and blue letters
73 Mend a seam, say
74 Sutcliffe of the early Beatles
75 Stage sign
76 Onetime host of "The Morning Show" and "The Tonight Show"
79 Iran-Iraq war weapon
81 In the ___, there's the greatest concentration of ___
85 Latin word on a cornerstone
86 That isn't it
87 Actress Kelly
88 Grim, as a situation
89 Dogfight enclosure
90 "Get Smart" group
91 In a ___, many a ___ is rolled
93 Rejecters of modern technology
95 Advance again
97 Co. that created the term "Buddy List"
98 In a ___, there's lots of ___ in the machinery
100 Lengthy time units
102 Spritzer mixer
106 R & B singer Marie
107 In ___, plenty of ___ is growing
111 In a ___, many a ___ is standing
114 Two-syllable unit
115 Aftershave sold in green bottles
116 Needle holder
117 Animal on Sri Lanka's flag
118 Stone used by pedicurists
119 Philosophies
120 Some Hindu music
121 Items sometimes seen on car tops
122 Sets forth

DOWN

1 Go from person to person?
2 Team building
3 When pigs fly
4 Occupy
5 With 51-Across, Caped Crusader portrayer
6 Site on St. Paul's first missionary journey
7 Violinist's need
8 Role in Verdi's "Falstaff"
9 Copper
10 He's flexible
11 Use a paper towel on
12 Punk music subgenre
13 Rule out
14 Bit of negative campaigning
15 Supporting structure
16 Measure of one's worth?
17 Easter Island mysteries
18 Oscar winner Lee
25 Bad lighting?
26 Setting of Margaret Mead's first book
28 Attacks with a lance
33 Collapse
34 Plant resembling Queen Anne's lace
35 Double curves
36 Missing persons
37 He-men's opposites
38 Cartoon feline
40 Looks hangdog
41 Burp
42 Tone
43 "Arabian Nights" monster
44 Mo. of Paul Revere's midnight ride
45 Nickname of Lincoln's youngest son
47 Make furrows in
51 Dam in a stream
52 Bit
54 Card game that uses jokers
60 Have bills to pay
61 Like fresh hay
63 Active from dawn to dusk
65 Guilder's replacement
66 Tough guy
67 Wine list column
69 Dark expression
70 War hero Murphy
71 Trifling
74 Nostalgic 1970's variety show
76 Large oval fruit
77 Short drawers?
78 Immunity provider
80 Onerous duty
82 Refinery input
83 Prefix with city
84 Chat room abbr.
87 Extinct kiwi kin
90 Turkic tribal leaders
91 Animals used as food on "Lost"
92 Dishes the dirt
94 Some linen
96 Raven-haired heroine of a Poe tale
99 Eye site
100 End of a ballade
101 Starts off
102 Highest, as honors
103 The way of the world?
104 Two in one's hand
105 Fools
108 Wrigglers
109 Composer Satie
110 Stretched
111 Grp. in TV's "Criminal Minds"
112 Sch. group
113 Prayer ___

by Patrick Berry

ACROSS

1 Most distant
7 Big Twelve team
13 Last of the Minor Prophets
20 First Ford
21 Philippine port
22 Nonrecurring publication
23 33.8 ounces?
25 Some honky-tonk music
26 Stephen of "The Crying Game"
27 Decoy site, maybe
28 Boil
30 Screen figure
31 Singers James and Jones
33 Friend of Dorothy, on "Sesame Street"
35 Disconnect
38 Stalwart plumber's credo?
43 Pharmaceutical chemist ___ Lilly
46 [Wham!]
47 End
48 Father of the Titans
50 Special attention, for short
53 Al ___
56 Ratchets (up)
57 Spoken
58 Pros
60 Teetotaling nun?
63 Straight
64 Saint in Brazil
66 Pops
67 Prefix with comic
69 Lawn tool
70 Long ago, long ago
71 Fur, e.g.
74 ___ Blaster (classic arcade game)
77 "Se ___ inglés?"
79 Make a bad copy of?
80 Winner's cry
81 Fiddle (around)
83 Oddly colored shoe?
88 Tide type
89 One line at passport control
91 U.S. highway with a ferry connection between Delaware and New Jersey
92 Language of India
94 Parts of apts.
95 Karate teacher
96 San ___, Tex.
98 Neth. neighbor
100 ___ rose
101 What the wet, baggage-laden passenger might take at the train station?
108 Former British royal
110 Newcastle's river
111 Old print
112 Actress Lena
114 And others
118 Calls a game
120 Western setting: Abbr.
121 One on the left
124 The ram in "A ram walks into a bar . . ."?
127 Rich green
128 Abet, in a way
129 Contract-negotiating pro
130 Garments at a 44-Down
131 Certain smokes
132 Chargers

DOWN

1 Eastern inn
2 Approaches in the Bible?
3 Think
4 Ending with how
5 Sloppy
6 Kind of shell
7 Light
8 Word before, after ___ or both before and after ___ "in"
9 Harmful
10 Spot
11 On the safe side
12 Kind
13 Oscar winner for "West Side Story"
14 Something to give an Alabama cheerleader?
15 Race part
16 John of "Freaky Friday," 1977
17 Rooster?
18 Human genus
19 Highway damaged by hurricane Katrina
24 Again
29 Most imposing
32 Venom carrier
34 Film character whose first name is Longfellow
36 Home of "Winged Victory"
37 About
39 Is into
40 Home of the N.C.A.A.'s Minutemen
41 California's ___ Valley
42 Recipe amts.
44 Outdoor party
45 Place for a 44-Down
49 Craftsperson
50 Enter
51 Aid for a detective
52 Like some C.S.I. evidence?
54 Game show contestant's option
55 Way to the top
59 Dirtbags
61 No-goodnik
62 Respect
65 Venus or Mars
68 Unit of hope?
71 Whisper sweet nothings
72 Dais delivery
73 Film company
75 Stray
76 "Not good!"
78 Behind
79 Quick
81 Quick
82 Title apiarist of film
84 Peeved
85 Soave or Orvieto
86 Bldg. planner
87 World capital on a gulf of the same name
90 At hand
93 Healthful food claim
97 1970 #1 song and album
99 Rd.
102 Investors' info
103 Hardens
104 Captain of the Nautilus
105 Fight
106 Put on the line
107 Mums
109 Month before febrero
112 Praise for toreadors
113 Home of the oldest university in the continental Americas
115 Lincoln and others
116 ___ Park, old Coney Island attraction
117 Emphasized: Abbr.
119 NCO's charges
122 Tore
123 Some H.S. math
125 American ___
126 Mr. Average

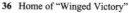

by Tony Orbach

ACROSS

1 Prefix with -drome
5 Mogul
9 Philippine seaport
15 Mug
19 Low part of a hand
20 Pickup shtick?
21 "Haven't a clue!"
22 Duck: Ger.
23 Base leader
25 Parisian entertainment since 1869
27 "Likewise"
28 Shackles
30 Juicy, tart apple
31 It may be pushed before starting
32 Homestead Act unit
34 Sponsor at Indy
36 1 + 1 = 3, e.g.
37 River of Hesse
38 British ___
39 Western Hemisphere grp.
41 ___-Foy, Québec
42 "Time to go now!"
47 Pause that refreshes
50 Phrase of nonspecific attribution
52 Leaked, as from a container
54 Nashville-based awards org.
55 Diamond baron Cecil
56 1998 animated bug film
57 Nymph pursuers
59 "___ the ramparts . . ."
60 Tasting of wood, as some wines
63 Itch cause
67 Like some cottage cheese
68 Friend in a sombrero
71 Household scare
73 Natural sparkler
74 Bakery order
75 Hells Canyon locale
76 Not to mention
78 Tuneful city "by the sea-o"
79 Brought up the rear?
81 Stir up
83 Guiding light
86 Prince Valiant's firstborn
87 Directional aid
91 Teeth, slangily
93 L.A. hours
94 Slicker, umbrella, galoshes, etc.
96 Opening sound?
99 It's in the genes
100 Places for laces
101 Lure
105 Elevator stop
107 MoMA's home
109 Lifts
110 "Amadeus" star Tom
111 Steamed dishes
113 Place of sacrifice
115 "Ulysses" setting
116 Christmas decoration site
118 He was no dummy
121 Trojan ally in the "Iliad"
122 Sci-fi weaponry
123 Jean ___, creator of 56-Down
124 ___-majesté
125 Plain and simple
126 Does a dog trick
127 "This is going to get ___"
128 ___'acte

DOWN

1 It's worn
2 Worn
3 Rest
4 Place for pearls
5 Classic Liz Taylor part
6 President of Pakistan, 1978–88
7 Lily Tomlin's Edith ___
8 Many a Floridian
9 Skinny
10 Nutcases
11 Heater with a storage tank
12 Exiled Amin
13 Historic Virginia family
14 Kilns
15 Edvard Grieg work
16 Quick-acting intl. military unit
17 Dogie
18 Witnessed
24 Rye fungus
26 Raises a howl
29 Lean against
32 Screened terrier
33 White-collar workers?
35 No longer owed
38 Linda Ronstadt's "___ Easy"
40 ___-Cat
43 See here!
44 Some bedtime reading
45 Nelson in reruns
46 Onetime American Communist leader ___ Hall
48 Uncommon sources of music nowadays
49 Stick to
50 Setting for some Sherlock Holmes mysteries
51 Combining of companies making the same product
53 Zest
55 Travel guide
56 "The Clan of the Cave Bear" heroine
58 One little piggy
61 Bee: Prefix
62 On the canvas, informally
64 Lab vessel
65 Immigrant's course: Abbr.
66 Network on a 55-Down: Abbr.
69 Atty. ___
70 They're easy to dial on a rotary phone
72 Chuck
77 Winds in a pit
80 "What's the ___?"
82 Lake that's a source of the Mississippi
84 Big time
85 Potential lifesaver for a drowning person
88 Mars or Mercury
89 Ex-senator Sam
90 Site of swings and a sandbox
91 Restaurant chain founded in 1958 near L.A.
92 Edges
95 "Nothing is so much to be feared as fear" penner
97 Croaking
98 Boring result
102 It may lead to a breakout
103 Least friendly
104 Two fins' worth
105 Three-time N.F.L. M.V.P., 1995–97
106 Staggers
108 Bob Cratchit, in "A Christmas Carol"
110 "Ben-___"
111 Mets, Jets or Nets
112 Spur-of-the-moment
114 "___ of the D'Urbervilles"
115 Big John of golf
117 Literary monogram
119 Grooved on
120 Set

by Manny Nosowsky

ACROSS

1 Percussion instrument
5 Hive makers
11 Easily passed
15 Junket
19 "Oh, uh-huh"
20 One with a mortgage
21 Dark region of the moon
22 Do followers
23 Meat, lettuce, cheese and tomato in a foot-long bun?
25 Huge
26 Destructive 1995 hurricane
27 Glare reducer
28 Graffiti on a jail wall?
31 Traffic monitors
36 O.K.
37 "P.U.!"
38 Actor Charleson of "Chariots of Fire"
39 Poplar tree
40 Lifeguard's purview
43 Like some penguin feet
45 Social activity on a military base?
47 Pastor who pitches?
49 Prefix with light
50 Irritated with
52 Nascar circuits
53 Early second-century year
56 Something struck
59 Legal
63 Support payment query?
70 Cataract site
71 Refrigerator brand
72 "Finding ___"
73 Cinnamon source
74 Tidewater collector
75 Director Gus Van ___
76 Amounts owed at a diner?
79 "CHiPs" star of 1970's–80's TV
82 Snowmobile steerer
83 Obsessed with
84 Defense initiative, for short
86 Bad musician's "body part"
91 Draft org.
94 Part voting aye?
99 Headwear for a building chief?
102 "S O S"
103 Bottle size
105 Cat-___-tails
106 Maria preceder
107 Dockworkers' org.
109 Shine, in product names
110 Island hoppers
112 Junk mail a trucker might get?
116 Auto needs
117 Killarney's land
118 Drink mixer
119 Where we be?
125 Insurer's calculation
126 Bygone despot
127 One who's left
128 Big source of corn
129 Legis. meeting
130 Radio, e.g.
131 Judge's declaration
132 Run things

DOWN

1 Dogfaces
2 Big Ten powerhouse, for short
3 Homestead Natl. Monument locale
4 Unified whole
5 Looie or hooey, e.g.
6 Approached
7 "Then what?"
8 Food label fig.
9 Chicago futures exchange, for short
10 Arizona tourist town
11 Changed
12 Pitch-raising guitar device
13 Verdi aria
14 Having all angles equal to 144 degrees
15 Counselor on "Star Trek: T.N.G."
16 Fix, as brickwork
17 "Somehow everything gets done"
18 Footed glass
24 Clichéd
29 Romance novelist Roberts
30 Electrification
31 Totally consumed
32 "Take ___" ("Congratulations!")
33 Extra capsule in a pill bottle
34 Film style
35 Loudness measure
41 N.Y.C. landing site
42 Latin 101 word
44 Not quite rhyming
46 "Just ___ about to . . ."
48 Trump daughter
51 Robert Burns's "___ Louse"
54 "The Sound of Music" family name
55 Philanthropist Hogg
57 "What'll ___?"
58 When repeated, start of a child's taunt
60 Where the first Ringling Brothers circus was staged, 1884
61 Nobelist Wiesel
62 Places to put your feet up
63 Facility
64 Kind of tree
65 Having parts to be filled
66 "The Matrix" hero
67 Radio iconoclast
68 Bop
69 Ball
74 Outlaw
77 Small songbird
78 One way to the Hamptons, for short
80 The first letter in 84-Across
81 Bums
85 Uruguayan uncle
87 "Woe ___" (humorous grammar book)
88 Loco
89 Sport with arm-waving
90 Bubble makers
92 Fish throwaway
93 God with a crested helmet and spear
94 Sci-fi weaponry
95 It might end with a start
96 Rebels of the Southeastern Conference
97 Wary
98 Dudley Do-Right's love
100 Vital Russian route
101 Agitated
104 Stevedore
108 Emerged
111 Things counted by the second?
113 Signs
114 Genealogist's study
115 Nature film?
120 [per the original]
121 Size bigger than med.
122 It might be called in
123 Wise one
124 Rob Roy's refusal

by Patrick Merrell

ACROSS

1 Many applications
5 Miss
9 Tudor queen, informally
13 Rafting area
19 Final, e.g.
20 To be played in unison
21 Horse ridden by Hotspur in "King Henry IV, Part I"
22 Shrewdness
23 Jazzy James
24 Breakdown on a Hyundai assembly line?
27 Edit for TV, say
29 Birthplace of 41-Across: Abbr.
30 Reason for a flood of calls to the police dept., maybe
31 "Wheel of Fortune" purchase
32 Rev. Jesse on Sundays?
38 ___ florentine
39 Author Bagnold
40 Till bill
41 "Nemesis" novelist
45 Stickers
47 Old Roman's boast after a deer hunt?
52 Town north of Anaheim
53 Seat of Washoe County, Nev.
54 Runners at the corners, say, in baseball
55 Chow
56 Long in the tooth
57 Go on stage
59 Bluish gray
62 "Oh, give ___ home . . ."
63 Check for typos, e.g.
65 Some of Shakespeare's income?
69 Astroturf alternative
72 Truss
73 Popular vodka, informally
74 Newly mortared bricks and stones?
79 Decrees
83 With 74-Down, unanimity
84 Grisham's "___ to Kill"
85 Obstruct
88 Become unhinged
89 Words of confidence
91 Go ___ (start fighting)
94 Person making unauthorized reports
95 Oscar-winning Irene
96 November through April, to vacationers?
100 World Series game
101 Decorate with pointy figures
102 Unveil, in poetry
103 Instance
105 Mad staff: Abbr.
106 One needed to bestow a blessing on a golf club?
112 Leaves at a luau
114 Mad., e.g.
115 1950 World Cup host, with a stadium for 180,000+ people
116 Musical with the song "N.Y.C."
117 Advice to Claudius, in "Hamlet"?
123 Memorable 2004 hurricane
125 Spoke in a poke?
126 Spoils
127 Dubai or Houston
128 TV part
129 Gets rid of
130 Big petrol seller
131 Chop ___
132 Formerly, once

DOWN

1 "Is that a fact?!"
2 Supersized
3 Phase of life before retirement
4 Buss
5 "Beauty and the Beast" role
6 Words said with a raised hand
7 Reward for going home?
8 Pick up
9 Most insolent
10 Volkswagen model
11 Took notice
12 State of confusion
13 Far out
14 Coolers, for short
15 Commonly accepted as such
16 Comment after looking at one's cards
17 Submarine base?
18 NBC inits.
25 ___-frutti
26 Cambodia's Lon ___
28 Applications
32 N.B.A. legend Kareem Abdul-___
33 Oscar winner for "Separate Tables"
34 Driver's lic., e.g.
35 Adequate, old-style
36 Tablet
37 See 117-Down

42 Home of El Nuevo Herald
43 Wedding band, maybe
44 Travel items
46 Dishonest sort
48 Rejections
49 Jet part
50 Battery number
51 Out of place
53 Pharaoh, for one
58 ___-Rooter
60 Company on the move
61 Yellow ball
64 "Di quella pira," e.g.
66 Palindromic writer
67 Eggheady sort
68 Flop
70 Hit hard
71 Where "yes" is "ioe," pronounced in three syllables
74 See 83-Across
75 Like the emperor Atahualpa
76 Backs
77 Like baseball covers
78 Thanksgiving dishes
80 It starts in Yellowstone National Park
81 Barrel-shaped marine mammals
82 Meager
86 Sponge

87 Long bones
90 Splits hairs
92 On and after
93 Be under, as an officer
97 Ewe said it
98 Cold response?
99 High point
100 V.I.P.'s opposite
104 Meager
107 Africa's ___ Tomé
108 Future seed
109 ___ Circus (ancient Roman arena)
110 Big name in trading cards
111 Put together
112 Hidey-hole
113 10,900-foot European peak
117 With 37-Down, popular book on grammar
118 Laugh syllable
119 Tailback's stat: Abbr.
120 Call for help
121 Symbol of worthlessness
122 It's found in seams
124 Celtic rival

by David J. Kahn

ACROSS

1 Sharp cheese quality
4 Center of emotions
9 Mountain top?
15 ___ Club of old TV
18 Big record co.
19 Many, many
21 This puzzle's northern border?
22 Be in a hole
23 Access code?
25 Stockpiles
26 Fired up
27 Scruffs
28 Its clue reads "Unstable subatomic particle"
30 Treater's words
32 Key-signature preceder
33 Family subdivisions
34 Opposite of post-
36 Drying chamber
37 With 33-Down, quickly
38 More than devotion
40 Sine ___ non
41 Gary ___, Pulitzer-winning Beat poet
42 Kind
43 Plays
44 Abrasive stuff
46 Spot for slop
47 Prevent from escaping
49 Breaches of faith
51 With 97-Across, bearer of edible triangular nuts
53 Land with monsoons
54 Not monaurally
58 Meat, in Madrid
61 Count with many titles
64 More faithful
65 Congresswoman Abzug and others
67 Vulnerable point
68 "Awww"-inspiring
69 It may be indicated by a stroke
70 Hot
72 An Untouchable
73 Mosaic flooring
75 Restaurateur Toots
76 Newport Beach sight
78 Where a bell ringer may stand
80 Ibsen play
83 Like some carol apparel
86 Within reach
87 Receiver's counterpart
90 Gave birth to
92 Drops
94 Fourth of 12: Abbr.
95 Eye openers?
96 Clark of country music
97 See 51-Across
98 Provided, as a line
99 ___ haddie (smoked fish)
100 Run for dear life?
102 Cold war draft
104 Williams's "Popeye" co-star
105 Attacked in a rage
106 Unpaired
107 Missed a golden opportunity
110 Disagrees
113 In shape
114 This puzzle's southern border?
115 Antarctica's ___ Coast
116 French pronoun
117 "___ bad!"
118 Hot
119 Water falls?
120 "___ a chance"

DOWN

1 It may glow in the dark
2 Crater creators, e.g.
3 Makeshift Frisbee
4 One taking a big bow
5 Suffix with Capri
6 Message in a bottle, maybe
7 Already chosen for play, say
8 Mass x velocity measurements
9 Sound in the middle of Italy
10 Unstable subatomic particle
11 Minute opening?
12 Beetle, e.g.
13 Hall-of-Fame pitcher Joss
14 Onetime
15 Spots for some shirts
16 Matching pair
17 "Here, maybe I can do it"
20 They're often dinged
24 Once called
29 Suffix with direct
31 RCA competitor
33 See 37-Across
34 Big name in sneakers
35 Like baba
39 Bay windows
40 Ancient Roman financial officer: Var.
41 Targeted, as with a mailing
44 Boom
45 Firms: Abbr.
48 "Sic et Non" author
49 Discuss business at a social occasion
50 Mansion staff
52 Bay
53 Hater
55 Rustic
56 Often-smoked fish
57 Metallurgists' supplies
58 Explorer at Labrador in 1497
59 French conductor Leibowitz
60 Red or Card
62 Satellite of 1962
63 Approval on "The Little Rascals"
66 Strong women
68 Licentious man
70 Blood carriers
71 Has trouble swallowing
74 Place of chaos
77 Cow annoyers
79 Org. in TV's "Nash Bridges"
81 Adds as a bonus
82 State capital on the Tietê River
83 Started to melt
84 Home of many talk shows
85 Opposite of dominate
87 Supplier of candy and toys for kids
88 "Shane" actor
89 Lion, at times
91 It's used to check septic systems
93 Asian observance
95 Shareholder's income: Abbr.
98 Steakhouse selection
99 Cot alternative
101 Guitar great ___ Paul
103 They were once cloned
104 Chop up
108 Prefix with skeleton
109 Actor Wheaton
111 Yalie
112 Take in slowly

by Joe DiPietro

ACROSS

1 Relaxed
8 Co. that makes Band-Aids
13 Pivots
19 Dish ladled out hot or cold
20 Draw out
22 Dominant dogs
23 In myth, killer of his own mother, Clytemnestra
24 Chinese symbols on Santa's vehicle?
26 Do some tailoring
27 Snooker need
28 Fortuneteller's opening
29 Baseball's Moises
30 Paleontological wonder at a natural history museum
31 Part of old French Indochina
33 Punching devices
35 "March of the Penguins" director ___ Jacquet
36 8-Down, with "the"
37 Rolling rock
38 Itsy-bitsy door decoration?
43 Like some chiefs
45 Variety
46 Second string
47 Refuges
49 Spoke at great length
52 1994 sci-fi writer's memoir
56 Makings of a coup
57 Some 1960's coupes
58 "Get ___ get out"
60 Chemical ending
61 Home's counterpart
63 Sold out, in a way
67 In use
69 Hearst's San ___ castle
70 Delay
71 Scratch
72 Tremor
73 Relief provider
74 Dispatch boats
75 Spigot site
76 Common green house gift
77 A long, long time
79 "___ Rollo" (popular Mexican variety show)
80 Big test
83 Opposite of should
87 Whitish
88 "Don't get any ___"
90 ___-Caps
91 Hot dog
93 Sunburnt Santa?
97 Greek height
98 Dandy
101 River of Devon
102 Kind of terrier
103 ___ speak
104 Bog down
105 Big top?
107 Sight from Messina
109 It might leave tracks
110 "Peter Pan" writer
112 Santa reindeer-turned-zombie?
116 Fetch
117 Three in one
118 Celebrates
119 Woman in Sartre's "No Exit"
120 Texas city
121 Goodwill
122 Sauntered

DOWN

1 Cancels
2 One who might grab the bull by the horns
3 Gifts you only think about giving?
4 Hedingham Castle locale
5 Court minutes
6 Place to get a reaction in school?
7 Venusians, e.g.
8 Manger figure
9 Everything, on the Ems
10 Never, in Nürnberg
11 Early seventh-century year
12 Christmas gift easily identifiable by shaking?
13 Away's partner
14 Suffix with form
15 Kraft Nabisco Championship org.
16 Spiny cactus
17 Expired
18 Per se
21 Amazon's home
25 Cross-out
27 Handler of gifts for the kids on the "naughty" list?
32 Call at sea
34 Attest
37 Fleur-de-___
38 Mincemeat ___
39 Corner piece
40 Stretch (out)
41 Dorm overseers, for short
42 Popular record label
44 Adjusts, as laces
47 Pogo, e.g.
48 Italian tragic poet Vittorio
50 Stern parent's reply
51 Played some songs, say
53 Throws a Christmas tree?
54 "Encore!"
55 Hunter's meat
57 Star wearer: Abbr.
59 Christmas quaffs set atop a board?
62 Dot follower
64 Film buff's cable channel
65 Thrice, in Rx's
66 Grp. with the 1977 hit "Do Ya"
67 "Mazel ___!"
68 Melodic pieces
71 "Law & Order" figs.
73 Sell to a new audience, say
76 Rescues
78 Military trial, briefly
81 "___ the season to be jolly"
82 N.J. summer setting
84 G8 member
85 Serengeti grazer
86 Christmas laughs
87 Tokyo-based carrier
89 Father Time prop
92 1962 Paul Anka hit
93 Precede
94 Stephen Hawking's alma mater
95 Comedian ___ Mac
96 Kansas City suburb
99 Brooks Robinson, e.g.
100 Squinted (at)
103 Like dishwater
104 1957 hit for the Bobbettes
106 Obligation
108 Genesis man
109 QB Hasselbeck
111 Hgts.
113 U.S.N. officer
114 Stephen of "V for Vendetta"
115 Samuel's teacher, in the Bible
116 Two qtrs.

by Brendan Emmett Quigley

FILM PARADE

ACROSS

1 Sharp competitor
4 "Do ___ to eat a peach?": Eliot
9 German link
12 Represent, as in legal matters
18 Ectomorphic
19 Worker with a chair
20 Be a make-up artist?
21 Red fluorescent dye: Var.
22 1954 film set in 16th-century Japan
24 Old cable inits.
25 They may get into a jam
26 Low digits
27 Elite groups
29 About
30 Many garden plantings
32 Most broad?
34 Wide shoe spec
37 1981 Alan Alda comedy, with "The"
42 Underground network
43 Diplomat Silas
45 Flip (out)
46 Jubilant
48 Barely beat
49 Director Welles
50 Stockholm flier
51 1982 Dudley Moore tearjerker
54 British gun
55 In a sardonic way
56 Blood line
57 Goldman ___
59 Pre-Q queue
60 Some accents
63 Bad beginning?
66 Prof.'s helpers
67 More manly-chested
70 Charged
71 "Yeah, that'll happen!"
73 "All the Things You Are" composer
74 Avian meat
75 Wordsworth works
76 1983 Charles Bronson thriller
79 Symbol
80 Fed. medical research group
81 Fey of "30 Rock"
82 Supremos
83 QB Favre
84 Child's activity?
86 Candy holder
87 Madrid Mrs.
88 Browns slowly
90 Roman man
91 "___ new?"
93 Fights
94 Pang
96 Tale
97 1990 sequel to "Chinatown," with "The"
101 Half of a 1955 merger: Abbr.
104 January 1 events
105 Colorado Indian
106 Ghost
107 Instruments with keys
109 Off
110 Christopher who wrote "Still Me"
112 1988 baseball flick
115 Emeritus: Abbr.
116 In an odd way
119 Magazine success
120 Cart
122 Subscription card option
127 Feminine suffix
128 The Caribbean's ___ Islands
130 Suffix with glass
131 1987 Peter Falk crime caper
133 "Quantum Healing" author
134 Some linemen: Abbr.
135 Heraldic silver
136 Towel embroidery
137 Reasons
138 Summer clock setting: Abbr.
139 Entangle
140 Gridiron figs.

DOWN

1 Incomes
2 Pause in verse
3 Cape ___, Mass.
4 "___ Said" (Neil Diamond hit)
5 Knock out, say
6 Start of a spell
7 Tail end
8 "Love Story" author Segal
9 Last month
10 1995 Hugh Grant farce
11 Rock stats
12 Auspices
13 With 81-Down, tradition suggested by this puzzle's theme
14 Bygone despot
15 1970 Jack Nicholson picture
16 ___ lark
17 Thing in court
18 Original title of Beethoven's "Fidelio"
19 Rafter's wood
22 Crooks
23 Dover delicacy
28 Not liquidy
31 Begins courting
33 Cable staple since 1979
35 Organic compound
36 Choosing-up word
38 "___ needle pulling thread" ("The Sound of Music" lyric)
39 Flamenco cheer
40 Rob Roy's refusal
41 Co. shares
44 Overthrowing, e.g.
47 Twisty curve
52 Temper
53 Old IBM PC's
54 Price reader
56 Turkish V.I.P.'s
58 Feuding (with)
59 Gas station adjunct, often
60 It may go for a couple of bucks
61 Dashboard feature
62 1932 romance with Maurice Chevalier
63 Actor with a mohawk
64 Kind of harp
65 Elegy
67 Laugh sound
68 Not play it straight
69 Peewees
71 Kind of test
72 War stat
73 Metric wts.
76 Baseball's Martinez
77 Part of E.S.L.: Abbr.
78 Bank offering
79 It's surrounded by white
81 See 13-Down
83 Some cricketers
85 Popular smokes
86 1999 film set in the Persian Gulf
88 ___ choy
89 Parisian way
91 Flamingo, e.g.
92 Speedway letters
93 Huge financial loss
94 It'll give you a lift
95 Instruction to a chauffeur
96 Gagarin in space
98 Golf's Michelle
99 ". . . ___ quit!"
100 Springy dance
101 Joint proprietors
102 Cold-blooded pets
103 Horse handler
106 Unload
108 Like a Cyclops
111 Most loathsome
113 1545 council site
114 No more than
117 Arm parts
118 Jewish orgs.
121 Concert gear
123 Bring in
124 Org. for women drivers
125 Copycat
126 Actress Daly
128 Junk bond rating
129 "I see!"
132 "___ me?"

by Elizabeth C. Gorski

ACROSS

1 Cross, maybe
6 Met expectations?
11 Refuge
20 Nitrogen compound
21 TV exec Arledge
22 Last czarina of Russia
23 "Absolutely, ambassador"
25 Colonies, e.g.
26 Frigid
27 Southern group address
28 Alliance dissolved in 1977
29 "Wonderful!"
30 Pulitzer Prize subj.
32 Continental capital
34 Starter: Abbr.
36 Island with a Hindu majority
39 Like some unpopular leaders
45 Computer pioneer Lovelace and others
48 The Huskies of the N.C.A.A.
50 Fraternity letters
51 Captivate
52 Antivenins, e.g.
53 Award-winning TV host
56 Charles Lindbergh, once
58 Buzzer
59 Blue-pencil
60 Advance
62 Academy head
63 Follower of mars
64 Modern greeting
66 Narrow the gap with
67 Marine mammal
70 Advantageousness
71 Fair fare
72 Friends
73 Went downhill
74 "___ ramparts!"
75 St.-Tropez's Place des ___
76 Bingo call
77 Cuneiform discovery site
79 Cartesian conclusion
82 "It's dark in here!"
84 x
86 Ad time
87 Main international airport of Japan
91 Width measure
92 Holy text
93 Raison d'___
94 1+1=2, e.g.
97 Great American Ball Park team
98 Death on the Nile cause, perhaps
100 "Brave New World" drug
101 Usher in
103 ___-Boy
105 Keep an ___ the ground
109 Some Wall St. deals
112 Daughter of Zeus
116 Claim
118 Weighty issue?
120 Scoots over
121 Prudential competitor
122 Female demon
123 Nickname for Tasmania
124 Waste
125 City on the Rhone

DOWN

1 "Apocalypto" subject
2 Like some profs.
3 Wink in tiddlywinks, e.g.
4 "Take your pick"
5 Sainted pope of 682
6 Airport sign abbr.
7 Classic theater name
8 Seat of Allen County, Kan.
9 Shaker leader
10 Shut off
11 Dirge
12 Natural balm
13 Relief provider, for short
14 Out
15 Capital once known as Thang Long ("Ascending Dragon")
16 Cuckoo bird
17 Streaming content
18 Composer Dohnányi
19 Ambassador or Statesman of old autodom
24 Campus 100 miles NW of L.A.
31 Hip
33 Oysters ___ season
35 Molotov cocktail component
36 Onion, for one
37 Teen trouble
38 Treasure-trove
40 Not built up
41 Tiny time unit: Abbr.
42 Capacitance measure
43 Richard of old westerns and action films
44 Pentagon fig.
46 Playground retort
47 It's a wrap
49 Most gutsy
54 ___ Circus (where St. Peter was crucified)
55 Enter
57 Fictional knight named for a bird of prey
60 Carriage
61 Fabulous monster
63 Property recipients
65 Do, re, mi
66 "I've ___ Strings" (Pinocchio song)
67 Like tears
68 Bring out
69 Rare ex-prisoner
70 Classic Jaguar
71 Some horns
73 Brooking no dissent
74 Lead-in to bow or hike
76 Show pride, in a way
78 Memory: Prefix
79 About
80 Just barely
81 Much of Colo.
83 "Mad TV" rival, for short
85 Marin and Sonoma's region
88 "I'll get this"
89 Chinese "way"
90 Two bags of groceries, say
95 Talk on and on, Down Under
96 Get wind of
99 Intrinsically
102 Ringlike formation
103 Priest of the East
104 "Pronto"
106 Longfellow's bell town
107 Paraguay and others
108 Cleaver or lever
110 Numerical prefix
111 RR stops
113 Sailor's saint
114 Ruhr refusal
115 Latin 101 verb
117 Reef dweller
119 Not abroad

by Ashish Vengsarkar

28 SOUNDS OF OLD

ACROSS

1 Eponymous physicist
6 Mary Kay rival
10 See 64-Down
14 Corroborator, maybe
19 Drink
20 Ill humor
21 Online initialism
22 Parts of a routine
23 Hat with a plume
24 Steady, say
25 Family-gathering time
26 One year's record
27 Like shoes made in St. Louis and finished in New Orleans?
31 "Bambi" character
32 Tops
33 2001's "Ocean's Eleven" and others
34 Matching
35 Bear witness
38 Fauna
40 Listing
42 Part of a parka
43 Detroit's Joe Louis ___
44 "Gr-r-ross!"
45 Old pigskin org.
46 Got a facial piercing?
51 Danger to divers
54 Birthplace of the Cyrillic alphabet
56 Dressing room door figure
57 "Funny Girl" composer
59 Dadaist Max
60 Flips
63 Acclaim
64 Got by
66 Crooks on golf courses
67 Kind of iron
68 Moon of Uranus
69 Diver's hose
70 "Blood and Fire" for the Salvation Army
71 Certain finish
72 Break
73 Bread-for-cake event?
76 Tie indicator
77 Played tenpins in officers' uniforms?
82 Good deal
83 ___ Falls
85 Hides a mike on
86 Fair shelter
87 Modern site of the capital of ancient Galatia
89 Pinkish yellow
92 Deepen
94 Home paper
95 Freshly consider
97 French word of approval
98 Sacrifice fly stat
99 Walking on hot embers?
105 Top
107 Bothers
108 Familiar sigh
109 Boy in TV's "Life Goes On"
110 Old war story
111 Tennis's Nastase
112 Jell-O flavor
113 Boring bit
114 To-do list
115 Org. in TV's "Adam 12"
116 Ankh feature
117 Novel content

DOWN

1 Chuck
2 Parrot
3 SeaWorld frolicker
4 Silt locale
5 Some terminals
6 Superior's title
7 Pleasant hotel room feature
8 Pearl Buck heroine
9 Elementary particle
10 Screening locale
11 Making no value judgments
12 Some oil barons
13 Work out
14 Close to closed
15 First name in horror
16 Comment about suddenly thinner mares?
17 Small topper
18 Easter, e.g.
28 Schedule-shifting syst.
29 Atlas, e.g.
30 Opera singer Simon ___
34 Pampering, for short
35 Starring role for John Barrymore and Gregory Peck
36 Good source of protein
37 Rang true?
38 Painter's calculation
39 Actor Beatty
41 They just scrape the surface
43 Made a touchdown
44 Knight's time
46 Place to get a grip
47 Estimator's phrase
48 City north of Cologne
49 Oater transport
50 Is off guard
52 Hydroxyl compund
53 ___-majesté
55 Say hey to
58 University of Massachusetts
60 "Blame It on the Bossa Nova" singer, 1963
61 Like some bodies on a beach
62 Samuel's teacher, in the Bible
64 With 10-Across, popular 1960's–70's singer
65 Kazakhstan's ___ Sea
66 Combination lock feature
67 Cooking vessels
69 Part of a Lawrence Welk count
70 "Serpico" author
73 Writer Harte
74 Dragged out
75 Female name ending
78 Midwest transfer point
79 Causing wonder in
80 Line of soldiers needing medical attention
81 "My man!"
84 Little League coach, often
86 "Message received"
87 Nimble
88 Distant cloud
89 Fifth-century invader
90 Avant-garde composer Glass
91 Finished, as dishes
92 Game piece
93 Worker for tips
96 Sell online
97 Clean up, in a way
99 Mercury and Mars
100 Grant's birthplace
101 Magazine contents
102 Start of a conclusion
103 Barely gets, with "out"
104 Phoenician trading center
106 Former U.S. terr.

by Harvey Estes

ACROSS

1 Fly effortlessly
6 Bub
9 Unstable
14 Talks up
19 Raise the proof?
21 Think the world of
22 Muppet who sang "Rubber Duckie"
23 1956 Oscar-winning title role for Ingrid Bergman
24 James Stockdale as running mate?
26 Terse account of what happened at the Raptor Petting Zoo?
28 Remained functional
29 Vest wearers
30 Tightens a piece, say
31 Golfer Ballesteros
32 Kind of bar
34 Attended without really belonging
36 "The child of Pride," according to Jonathan Swift
37 Badge awarder: Abbr.
40 "___ go bragh!"
41 Girl who wears hair clips in nonstandard ways?
46 Stimpy's TV pal
47 Poet/novelist Elinor
48 Like a crow or lark
49 Morales of "NYPD Blue"
50 Half of a longtime country duo
52 Impetuous quality
53 Forbidding
54 Quite often
55 Subtly suggest
57 Sows with salt, maybe
58 Work on logical proofs while dining out?
63 Historic Irish city
64 Bête ___
65 Player's chance to shine
66 External
67 ___ of Oxford
68 Oscar nominee for "Unfaithful," 2002
73 "You said a mouthful!"
74 Archive's contents
76 Subsided
77 Alternative to Rover
78 Practice sessions for coercion?
81 Sprout
82 Infiltrator
83 "___ says?"
84 Suspicious
85 Tries
86 One of Emma's lovers in "Madame Bovary"
87 Quonset hut material
89 Lickety-split
90 In more pain
93 Show contempt for yellow fruit?
98 The Kingdom of Heaven?
100 About whom Shakespeare wrote "Age cannot wither her, nor custom stale / Her infinite variety"
101 Two-time loser to Dwight
102 Jive, e.g.
103 Kind of hat
104 Tranquility
105 Deep gulf
106 Geared up
107 Isn't complete without

DOWN

1 Seven-time Wimbledon winner
2 River of Yakutsk
3 "High Sierra" actress
4 Sony introduction of 1984
5 Impedes legally
6 Other: Abbr.
7 Inter ___
8 Crimson
9 Accesses
10 Lead-in to further explanation
11 Summer sweaters?
12 Impel to action
13 So far
14 City on the Seine
15 Cropped up
16 Hand or foot
17 They're spotted in casinos
18 Some bird feed
20 Whips but good
25 Split
27 Underground film actress Sedgwick
31 Main character in Proust's "Remembrance of Things Past"
32 Cousin of a gull
33 Vicinity
34 General acknowledgment?
35 Like the Gobi
37 Split, in a way
38 Horror film's offerings
39 Claude who starred in TV's "Lobo"
41 "Here's a pleasant surprise!"
42 Fly from Africa
43 Ceremonial splendor
44 Sporty Mazda
45 Another name for vitamin A
47 More artful
51 1984 Hollywood biopic
53 Like diplomatic pouches
55 Distinctive Rolls-Royce feature
56 Ending with profit or racket
57 Some reconnaissance craft
58 Foster, as enthusiasm
59 Bistro
60 Nonsensical
61 NBC newswoman O'Donnell
62 In a convenient way
63 Witches' familiars, often
67 "Conspiracy of Fools" topic
68 Cancels, as in an online order form
69 Steel grating component
70 "Metaphysica" writer
71 Swift production?
72 They've split
74 How things may get washed
75 Soup accompaniers
79 Ladylove
80 Go through volumes
81 Make larger or smaller, as a photo
85 Clavell novel set in Hong Kong
86 Pale purple
87 No-goodnik
88 Olympians Liddell and Heiden
89 Jumper
90 Order letters
91 Set of standards
92 ___ Bowl (postseason game)
93 Colorless
94 "Hard ___!" (sailor's yell)
95 Confined, with "up"
96 Walked along
97 ___-culotte
99 Cereal box abbr.

by Patrick Berry

ACROSS

1 Shoots
6 Wicker willow
11 Bee Gees brother
15 Cry from a butterfingers
19 Words sung "with love" in a 1967 hit
20 Band of fighters
21 ___ vez (again, in Spanish)
22 "Fudge!"
23 They may be pulled
25 It may be pulled
27 Visibly showed displeasure with
28 "Falstaff" and others
29 Contest of wills?
32 Member of the familia
34 Lady from Ipanema
38 Neutral shade
39 Half of a 1970's TV duo
43 Traveled (along)
44 Cookout staple
45 ___-mo
46 Goethe play
48 Cusp
49 One may be pulled
54 Scripture topic
55 Mil. mail drop
57 Appeared
58 Roasted snacks
60 Lincoln, maybe
63 Hibernation site
64 Water holder
65 Select group
67 Bank holdings
68 They may be pulled
70 Place for a beer and a bite
71 Stu of early TV
72 Dandy
73 She-demon
74 Like some Roman tragedies
75 Feature of many a hospital rooftop
77 Saw-edged
79 Day divs.
80 "___ see"
81 It may be pulled
85 Blockheads
87 Half of a 1980's TV duo
88 Sot's affliction
89 Lyndon Johnson, by birth
92 Fireplace receptacle
94 Brandy glass
97 Some jackets
98 Women's apparel department
100 "Count me out"
101 Convertibles
103 Fundamental figure in geometry
106 Tiger Beat topic
109 It may be pulled
112 They may be pulled
116 Pizazz
117 Always
118 Syrian leader
119 Grasshopper stage
120 Arab League member
121 Break off
122 Content of some rings
123 Far from enthusiastic

DOWN

1 Place to sell tkts.
2 Campaign pro
3 Immigrant's class: Abbr.
4 A hummingbird has a fast one
5 Country that styles itself a "democratic socialist republic"
6 Yellowish shade
7 Fill
8 Fingered, briefly
9 Text miscues
10 Not let settle
11 Kind of dancer
12 "Live ___!"
13 Highland hillsides
14 Hair clasps
15 Worthless loafer?
16 Sch. in Tulsa
17 Stroke
18 Dump
24 Hood's rod
26 Linda of soaps
29 Abbr. of politeness
30 Gradually slower, in mus.
31 It may be pulled
33 ___ as a fiddle
35 It may be pulled
36 University official
37 Gulf of ___, off the Horn of Africa
39 Diet
40 Worked out
41 "Krazy ___"
42 Desert bloomers
45 Chinese checkers board shape
47 Counterfeit
50 Some VCR's
51 Pushes off
52 They may be pulled
53 Köln's river
55 "Look ___!"
56 Oliver Twist's birthplace
59 Besides that
61 Pulitzer-winning writer Sheehan
62 Diogenes, for one
64 Put down
66 Major stretches
68 Posers
69 Prix de ___ de Triomphe (annual Paris horse race)
70 Kick
72 Strike out
74 Marie and others: Abbr.
76 Pilot, flight attendants, etc.
77 Lager holder
78 Observatory observer: Abbr.
80 Sharp rebuke
82 Diarist Anaïs
83 "Aha!"
84 1962 musical co-directed by Bob Fosse
86 Secretly watched
90 Econ. measure
91 C.I.A. ancestor
93 Swift's "A Tale of ___"
95 Mullahs' calls
96 Basic belief
99 Freedman, once
101 ___ Janeiro
102 Naval V.I.P.
104 Furniture retailer since 1943
105 Laura of "I Am Sam"
107 Petrol brand
108 Sask. neighbor
109 "Deadwood" carrier
110 Tentacle
111 Actress Long
113 Literary monogram
114 ___ Friday's
115 Brick holder

by Victor Fleming and Bruce Venzke

ACROSS

1 *Sweater option
6 *Choice cut
16 *Primo
20 ___ Nast magazines
21 "Hey, good lookin'!"
22 Prior work
23 ___-totsy
24 Construction toy
25 Rock music's Better Than ___
26 Serpent suffix
27 Mythical bird-woman
29 Works on
30 Roman fountain name
31 Executes
33 Acknowledge
34 Cheat
35 Some Ivy Leaguers
36 Philosopher Kierkegaard
37 Perfectly
38 Existing at birth
41 Always
42 Terse response to an interruption
46 Ties up
47 Symbol of speed
49 Author Silverstein
50 "___ not"
51 Section
52 Zero
53 Infamous innkeeper
55 Info on an electric bill
56 Rants
58 One doing the twist, e.g.
60 Deli order
61 What the answers to the 15 starred clues have
64 Summer hrs. in N.Y.
67 Lean
68 Biker's prop
72 Retired N.H.L. great Hull
74 Palm, say
75 Mock-scared cries
76 Mil. school
77 Years in old Rome
78 Inured (to)
79 Nonprofit?
80 Central courts
81 Sang on high?: Var.
83 Paramount
85 Unyielding
86 In order (to)
87 King or queen
88 Comedian Mort
89 "The Paper Chase" author John Jay ___ Jr.
92 Ill
93 Treat for a dog
97 Golf outing
98 Where St. Paul was shipwrecked, in Acts
99 Ballot listing
100 Quiz feature: Abbr.
101 Still
102 Period of future bliss
104 Motown singer Terrell
106 Scrubbed
107 Diet soda feature
108 Resting, say
109 *Backup for Dick Tracy
110 *Gridiron lineup
111 *Benjamin

DOWN

1 *Show stopper?
2 To whom a dictator answers
3 Word with an arrow
4 Cautious investments, for short
5 Places for Peeping Toms
6 Units of heat
7 Pats on the back?
8 Mind
9 Its slogan was once "Be there"
10 Diner sign
11 Trigger
12 Activate
13 Buddy of TV
14 Vigoda and Fortas
15 Kit ___
16 Campari and Cinzano
17 Goes slowly
18 Temerity
19 *In-box contents
28 Kalahari-like
30 Isley Brothers hit "___ Lady"
32 Its logo is a rearing horse
33 It's nothing
34 Shade of black
36 Like sororities, at times
37 Nowheresville
38 *Apple variety
39 Best-selling author Roberts
40 ___ War of 1899
42 Product in an orange box
43 Caulk
44 Villain who says "For I am nothing, if not critical"
45 *Natural history museum attraction
47 Some restaurant employees
48 Chosen
49 Umpire's call
52 ___ Kinnock, 1980's–90's British Labor Party leader
53 *Saloon floozie
54 Author Rand
55 Modern addresses
57 Part of M.I.T.: Abbr.
59 Battle of Fair ___, 1862
62 Open field
63 Majestic
64 *Fortune 500 company based in San Jose, Calif.
65 Villain who says "That's a Dom Perignon '55. It would be a pity to break it"
66 Gravitate
69 Israeli port
70 It's right at your fingertip
71 *Critical time
73 Gets blitzed
78 ___ Bator
79 ___-white
80 Fit
82 Follower of "O"
83 Important exam
84 Home of Spelman College
85 Put (away)
87 Higher up
88 Gobs
89 *Certain gasket
90 Corot painting "The Burning of ___"
91 Dieter's problem
92 Md.'s largest city
93 Villain who says "So you don't like spinach?"
94 1980's Stallone role
95 Not fulfilled
96 *It's usually not played much
98 Upset
99 Acapulco approval
102 French month
103 D.C. baseballer
105 Common female middle name

by Paul Guttormsson

ACROSS

1 Shooting marble
6 Cradle call
10 What I will follow
14 Mystery writers' awards
21 Printing process, briefly
22 North Sea feeder
23 Dramatic solo
24 Observant Mormons, e.g.
25 Scottish hillsides
26 With gusto
27 Tendon injury
28 Emotional traumas
29 Full of compassion
30 Hit hard
31 Pitchers' places
33 From memory
34 Writer Gogol
36 Midwest and Plains states, e.g.
38 Old tar's shipmates
40 Siberian river port
44 No longer hungry
45 Where it's at
46 Endurance, informally
47 Whitecap formation
48 Maj.'s superior
49 French white wine
51 Reddish-brown gems
52 Relatively robust
53 Magnanimous
56 Washington's profile is on it
58 Prevented
60 Old Aegean region
62 Get ___ (be rewarded at work)
63 Stumble upon
64 Enthusiast
65 Mary Hartman's TV hometown
67 Screened, as a patient
68 Swing
69 "Gilligan's Island" castaway
70 "MADtv" alternative
71 Dirty
73 "Mr. Mom" co-star
74 East Lansing sch.
77 1972 #1 Neil Young hit
81 Deli delicacy
82 Depresses
86 Free
88 Break ground?
89 Grainy finishes
91 Physicist Fermi
92 One can be educated
94 Strong
95 Pregnant woman, in obstetrics
97 Feminine fiend
99 Pulitzer-winning biographer Leon
100 Pilotless plane
101 1938 #1 hit composed by Hoagy Carmichael
103 Physical sound?
105 Lee's men
106 Ending with ranch
107 Crash-investigating org.
109 ___ 'acte
110 Versatile vehicle
111 Work like ___
112 Dental damage
113 White-collar work
117 She married Dick twice
119 Not yet showing signs of wear
121 Founder of analytic psychology
123 "The Producers" extra
124 On a par with
128 Valentine symbol
129 Get shot in a studio?
130 Ply with drink
131 Better at stand-up
132 Still having a shot to win
133 Lead-in periods
134 Concertedly
135 Haberdashery buy
136 14 for Si or 102 for No: Abbr.
137 Joins
138 Player of Santa in "Elf," 2003

DOWN

1 Composer Berg
2 "The ___ Left Behind Me" (Civil War tune)
3 Have ___ with
4 Where "sage in bloom is like perfume," in song
5 Dawn deity
6 Oscar-winning "Titanic" song by Celine Dion
7 It touches three oceans
8 Get to people emotionally
9 Suffix with station
10 Be consumed with envy
11 Dream interpreter
12 Composer ___ Carlo Menotti
13 Lacking sympathy
14 In essence
15 Bee Gees brothers
16 "It's worth ___"
17 1917 Frank Lloyd film
18 ". . . made ___ woman": Genesis
19 Deluge refuge
20 Draft inits.
30 Eastern European pork fat dish
31 Of the morning
32 Coll. fraternity with a skull-and-crossbones symbol
35 Shakespeare's "The Rape of ___"
37 Andean capital
39 Río de la Plata, e.g.
41 To a greater extent
42 In the dumps
43 U.K. distance measures
46 ___-da (pretentious)
48 Well-trained company?
50 Minimal money
51 Give rise to
52 After-dinner development
54 Ukr. neighbor
55 Sci-fi figures
57 Cell stuff that fabricates protein, for short
59 "Dr." with Grammys
61 Yonder
63 Very quick rotation meas.
66 Flub
68 eBay entry
69 Upper figure
71 "Help wanted" letters
72 Cosmonaut Makarov
73 Pays for oneself
74 Ravel's "___ Antique"
75 Fishhook line
76 Battleship inits.
77 1967 medical milestone
78 Drab shade
79 Meeting points
80 Like a mensch
81 Become smitten with
82 Blue state
83 Chemical suffix
84 Urban grid
85 Joseph Conrad classic
86 Stowe villain
87 Clothe
88 Sneaky laughs
89 Typing speed stat.
90 Tic-tac-toe win
93 Meat stamp inits.
96 Golden calf crafter
98 Jewelry designer Peretti
100 Sixers' #6
102 Where nairas are spent
104 Blood type, briefly
108 Quaint cry of surprise
111 Tenochtitlán resident
112 Slew
114 1980's screen slasher
115 Earth protector
116 Pernicious pet
118 Hip parts
120 Left
122 Like antiques
124 Immature newt
125 On the ___ vive
126 Évreux article
127 Sitcom planet
129 Church perch
130 Sound heard while shearing

by Mark Feldman

ACROSS

1 Treat for a dog
6 California's ___ Woods National Monument
10 Near eternity
15 Runner's place
19 Moses' brother
20 "___ cost to you!"
21 Civil War signature
22 Sinatra's "Meet Me at the ___"
23 Organisation des ___ Américains
24 Calls the shots?
25 Einstein's asset?
27 Acerbic rock/folk singer?
30 Plenty
31 Like some garages
32 Jim Palmer, notably
34 Graf ___
35 "___ Tu" (1974 hit)
37 Interminably
39 Shell alternative
43 Protest gone bad?
48 The Henry who founded the Tudor line
50 Faulkner character ___ Varner
51 Little ___
52 Manche's capital
53 15 minutes of tightrope walking and animal acts?
57 Sign up for more
60 By and by
62 1993 Super Bowl M.V.P.
63 Worked (up)
64 1986 self-titled soul album
66 Done in
68 Con
70 Magic words . . . or a hint to the other long answers in this puzzle
77 Fashion
78 Percolate
79 Heretofore
80 Doo-wop syllable
83 Copy illegally
86 Greeting with a salute
88 "Baloney!"
89 Certain NASA probes?
92 Not docked
94 In the know
95 Eastern royal
96 Way-off
97 Deer season hairdo?
101 End of an act, maybe
104 Person at court
106 France ___ (Parisian daily)
107 Library indexing abbr.
109 Engine capability, slangily
112 Not stay alert
116 Post-accident inquiry
120 Troupe of suspects from "The Fugitive"?
122 Tennessee offense and defense?
124 Lead-in to girl
125 "___ Dream" ("Lohengrin" piece)
126 Space: Prefix
127 Chocolate, e.g.
128 Fed
129 Fix, as a bow
130 Sore, with "off"
131 Ones picking up things?
132 Psychiatrist's appt.
133 Detect, in a way

DOWN

1 Modern workout system
2 Bring home?
3 Make a delivery
4 Saw
5 Tangle up
6 French film director Allégret
7 Unborn, after "in"
8 About to receive
9 "The Barber of Seville" composer
10 Sock pattern
11 Ending with ballad
12 Cooking staple
13 Certain tides
14 Cons
15 Airport worker
16 Cadger's request
17 Anthony Mann's "The Fall of the Roman Empire," e.g.
18 Any King Christian I–X
26 French flag color
28 Lady Jane and Zane
29 Blessings
33 Ballade ending
36 Onetime French fleet
38 Dagger
40 "Yow!"
41 Word in many a Nancy Drew title
42 Hops-drying oven
43 Boxer nicknamed "Hands of Stone"
44 Año starter
45 Good ___
46 Admission of defeat
47 "A Confederacy of Dunces" author
49 "___ come as no surprise . . ."
54 Title woman in a Woody Allen film
55 River rental
56 Sequentially
58 Dict. info
59 First name in comedy
61 Hammer user
65 Some German imports
67 Relative of -ian
69 Logical start?
71 Font feature
72 Where an echograph is used in measuring
73 Tricks are played in it
74 Words with house or move
75 Polite refusal
76 Soap time, maybe
80 Georgia and others, once: Abbr.
81 Sen. McCarthy ally
82 "___ of the Thousand Days" (1969 film)
84 Run ___ (owe)
85 Literally, "instruction"
87 Rings of plumerias, e.g.
90 Napa sight
91 Cut off
93 + part
98 Defeats, in a way
99 Beams
100 "No ___!"
102 ___ Society (English debating group)
103 Jumps
105 Hen cages
108 Tours can be found on it
110 Wonderland cake message
111 Sp. women
113 Devastate
114 Slowpoke
115 Citation of 1958
116 Rat follower?
117 Progress
118 Suffix with major
119 Orthopedic specialty
121 Staffs
123 What barotrauma affects

by David Kwong and Kevan Choset

ACROSS

1 Stick used to swat flies
6 Doesn't run
11 Senseless
15 Place to relax
18 Popular humor weekly, with "The"
19 Something to lay down
20 "___ Enchanted" (2004 movie)
21 Heap
22 Birdie beater
23 First mate's greeting?
25 Break off
26 Hawks
28 One after another
29 Jct. joiners
30 Sticker
31 "Wheel of Fortune" request
32 Actors Max and Max Jr.
33 Animal with a black-tipped tail
35 Tighty-whities
37 Word with "hand to hand" or "time to time"
39 Inventor's inits.
41 Show taped at Chicago's Harpo Studios
43 Ecdysiast Blaze and others
44 Charging, in a way
46 Reported mountain sightings
47 U.S. auditor
48 "Baudolino" novelist
49 Ahead
51 Layer of a bed
52 Year Constantine the Great became emperor
55 Family of things
56 First name in humor
57 Some Guggenheim works
59 Acoustic
60 Fed. health research agcy.
61 Many a Wall St. Journal subscriber
62 1970's HUD secretary Hills and namesakes
65 C8H8
67 With 56-Down, start of eight answers in this puzzle
69 Fill up
70 St. Clare's birthplace
71 "The Facts of Life" actress
72 Post-op area
74 Navel type
75 "See ya"
76 Snick and ___
77 Attention
78 Weber State University locale
79 Greek group
81 Showed to the foyer
83 Abbr. after Lincoln or Kennedy
84 Iron-___
85 Misrepresent
87 Display on a tray
89 Shaw's "___ and Cleopatra"
93 Deposit in a depository
94 Code word
95 "See ya"
96 Corrida charger
97 Old computer
99 Beat
101 Court grp.
103 Pizazz
104 Häagen-___
105 Even though
107 Part of 60-Across

109 Master
110 Marvel Comics supervillain
113 Root beer ingredient
115 Tarnish
116 See 104-Down
117 Kind of inspection
118 Greenland settlers
119 Hesitations
120 Cornerstone abbr.
121 "Shall we go?"
122 Aquarium buildup

DOWN

1 The Axis, once
2 Together
3 Neighbor of Chad
4 Popular Bach work for keyboard (1994, 1996, 1999, 2002)
5 Having no depth, in brief
6 Arizona Diamondbacks ballpark (1988)
7 Had the advantage
8 Commercial suffix
9 Florida's ___ Trail
10 Wretches
11 Opening in the North Pole?
12 Ray of "Battle Cry"
13 Weak spots
14 Pompom holder
15 Birding capital of New Zealand (2006)
16 It's often tied with a rubber band
17 Common connectors
19 Some agents, for short
24 Company that merged with Lockheed in 1995 (2001, 2003)
27 Knot holder
29 Words from Pope's "An Essay on Man" (1940, 1942–43, 1960–62, 1965–68, 1978)
30 Some shot
32 Time magazine 2005 co-Person of the Year
34 Miniature
36 Least robust
38 Roasted fowl (2005)
40 Hollywood biggie?
42 President who created the N.S.C.
45 Sirtaki dancer in a 1964 movie
50 Tropical rodent
52 Zorro's house
53 Batters take them
54 Futurists? (1990–93, 1997–98, 2000, 2004)
55 "Rocks"
56 See 67-Across
58 Lucid

63 Break ___ (go into sudden death)
64 Public
66 Moviedom's Long and Vardalos
68 Composer Camille Saint-___
69 Big ___
73 Western capital (1979–82, 1984)
76 Sign of worry
79 "The Silence of the Lambs" org.
80 Alamo mission?
82 Put on
83 Mobile home?
84 Davy Jones's locker
86 Airport fig.
88 Transitional land zone
90 Eschewing accompaniment
91 Waters fed by the Amu Darya
92 Old White House nickname
98 Sale places
100 Harshness
102 Word with china or dry
104 With 116-Across, saucy Aussie
106 Advanced
108 "There!"
110 "Hmmm"
111 Youth org. since 1910
112 Top
114 Naut. heading

by David J. Kahn

ACROSS

1 Likewise
6 Chipped in
11 __ II razor
15 Where to see "Monday Night Football"
19 Ryan of Hollywood
20 Big throw
21 One of the Castros
22 Pluck
23 *Where to find para in the dictionary
25 * . . . oatmeal . . .
27 Minnesota __
28 History chapters
29 Restriction on children, maybe
31 4 x 4, for short
32 Exam for a future D.A.
33 Link with
34 Head-scratcher
38 Independent country since June 5, 2006
40 * . . . Suita . . .
42 Sneeze causers, for some
45 Plant openings
46 * . . . Hancock . . .
49 Not fully formed
52 Speed: Abbr.
53 Like some Keats works
54 Part of the Treasury Dept.
55 Rival of Cassio
56 Apprised
58 "The Man Who Knew Too Much" actress, 1934
61 Remark that might get one in trouble
62 When "Dallas" aired for most of its run: Abbr.
63 Dictionary source for each asterisked clue in this puzzle
69 Slate workers, for short
70 Actress Kimberly of "Close to Home"
71 Shooting match?
72 Big cavity
75 Course related to physiol.
76 Volga feeder
77 Fashion designer Saab
78 __ Hill (R & B group)
79 Guidance system at sea
81 * . . . boar . . .
84 1981 German-language hit film
87 Talks monotonously
88 * . . . subscapular . . .
92 Model's job
96 "That's cheating!"
97 Daffy Duck and others
98 Spanish __
100 Call to a calf
101 1989 high-school film based on a song title
103 Charades player
104 Farming prefix
105 * . . . war dance . . .
108 * . . . ZZZ . . .
111 Unhappy chorus
112 Lincoln, maybe
113 Rainwear brand
114 Fervor
115 Old flames
116 Stallone and others
117 Medgar of Mississippi
118 Hit the top

DOWN

1 Pinhead
2 There from birth
3 Show uncertainty
4 Running things?
5 __ Miss
6 Now, in Nueva York
7 Unfamiliar with
8 A little night music?
9 Longoria of "Desperate Housewives"
10 Wrecks
11 Faithful about
12 Needed more
13 A3 maker
14 San __, Calif.
15 "I" problem
16 Abbr. before a Spanish surname
17 Stomach part
18 Extraordinary degree
24 Writer of "Gil Blas"
26 Leader of the All-Starr Band
30 Shampoo form
32 Bad witness
33 Sondheim protagonist
35 Jelly flavor
36 High hat
37 Subtitle starter, sometimes

39 Fabrics with elaborate designs
40 Boggy lands
41 Terre Haute sch.
43 Rustling sound
44 Broad, in a way
46 Cape settler
47 Old mythological work
48 Trollope's "Phineas __"
49 Assessor's figure
50 Votin' no on
51 Reverse
55 To wit
56 Take __ (swing hard)
57 Mallard cousins
59 Physiques, for short
60 Modem termini?
61 __ Games, quadrennial event since 1951
62 Monastic title
64 It's parallel to a radius
65 Opposite of yellow
66 Big do
67 Dignitary from Dubai
68 Lockbox document
72 Write a codicil
73 "Huzzah!"
74 Jazz's __ Lateef
76 One of the winds

79 Frank Sinatra said he had "the silkiest chops in the singing game"
80 Handicapper's hangout, for short
81 Wall St. figures
82 Spots
83 Something to be thankful for
85 Without support, in a way
86 Basket material
87 Place for a small table
89 Turbulent
90 Real estate ad section
91 CD-__
93 "See ya!"
94 N.H.L. trophy honoree
95 Able to do well
98 Member of the track team
99 Stockpile
102 Get the goods on
103 Parcel (out)
104 "Suppose they gave __ and nobody came?"
105 Japanese P.M. Shinzo __
106 "America's Most Wanted" airer
107 Small digit
109 Kind of lane
110 Inits. for a film buff

by Randolph Ross

ACROSS

1 Prefix with red
6 Denpasar is its capital
10 "Concord Hymn" writer's inits.
13 Green ___
19 Green, for instance
20 Christmas team
22 Trunk lines
23 Green 55-Down
26 "Me too"
27 Make messy
28 Enzyme ending
29 Gremlins and Pacers
33 Codger
34 Fella
36 Rat follower
38 A hero might have it
40 Box in many homes
41 Bracelet
44 Green 83-Down
49 Like
50 Trademarked chilled drink
51 Neighbor of Lanai
52 Live
54 Ding
56 Be listless
57 Lot of money
58 Channel for debates
60 Fast runners
63 Some socials
65 Corroding, with "into"
66 Green 58-Down
72 Cry from a balcony
73 Neat as ___
74 Legless creatures
75 Quarter of a deck
76 Skid row sounds
78 Yves's eve
80 Natural flavoring
84 His or her, to Henri
85 Computer connection
86 Destruction
89 The third of September
90 Green 8-Down
95 Cartoon character with a big nose
96 Mideast money
97 Old TV part
98 Map parts: Abbr.
99 Still
100 Kathryn of "Law & Order: Criminal Intent"
103 "Put it back in"
104 The sun
107 Utah city
109 Like turncoats
112 Green 13-Across
119 Tony-winning actress Martin
120 Inferior
121 Server of Norm, Cliff and Frasier, on "Cheers"
122 Not overdone
123 Stopover
124 Those caballeros
125 Cap sites

DOWN

1 "Eww!"
2 Dijon denial
3 Part of Dixie: Abbr.
4 Bird in the "Arabian Nights"
5 Sacred chests
6 Stomach settler
7 Correo ___ (airmail)
8 Green ___
9 About
10 Fix, as a rug
11 Early Chinese dynasty
12 Marine birds
13 First person indicator
14 Early colonizer of America
15 Great time
16 Mountain whose name in Greek means "I burn"
17 Hurdles for high schoolers, for short
18 Being, to Brutus
21 Furry-tailed rodents
24 Spa treatment
25 Tend to
29 Syrian president
30 Word before or after sugar
31 Scrub
32 Egg holder
35 Philosophical study of the universe
37 ___ Friday's
39 Bad start?
40 Mountain view
42 Not think things through first
43 Off course
45 Measure of light
46 Cold coat
47 Enemy: Abbr.
48 Start of many a city name
53 Some M.I.T. grads: Abbr.
55 Green ___
57 It's connected to a boom
58 Green ___
59 Hideaway
61 NASA's ___ Research Center
62 Old truck maker
64 Verdi's "___ tu"
65 ___ trip
66 Bone setters
67 End of an estimate
68 Close relative
69 Place with a moving line
70 Ship in 1898 headlines
71 Start of a supplication
76 Papal court
77 N.Y.C. subway line
79 One of the Wright brothers, for short
81 Center of entertainment
82 "The Cloister and the Hearth" author
83 Green ___
85 Kindergarten handicraft
86 Preparing for shipment
87 "Rah!"
88 E.E.C. part: Abbr.
91 Indian tourist destination on the Arabian Sea
92 They're not pro
93 Fade out
94 Loire laugh
100 Actress Lanchester and others
101 Repetitive musical piece
102 Storage units
104 Did laps
105 "Yikes!"
106 Actor Alan
108 Year in the middle of this century
110 Father
111 Need
113 One-fifth of quindici
114 Suffix with ball
115 Best-selling author Brown
116 "___ Sleep Comes Down to Soothe the Weary Eyes" (Dunbar poem)
117 "Rah!"
118 Points on a scale

by Eric Berlin

ACROSS

1 Home of the Natl. Hollerin' Contest
5 Spicy cuisine
9 Beat ___ horse
14 Complain
18 Tenant's desire
20 Really rough
22 As a refutation
23 Acquirers of lost property
24 Part of New Eng.
25 Bit of cheer
26 Major source of the narcotic qat
28 Plain ___
29 Words under Washington's picture
32 "American Justice" network
33 International retailer whose name is an acronym
35 Stolen
36 Former German president Johannes
37 Major finale?
39 Desert attribute
43 Co-star of "Blow," 2001
44 Noisy celebration
46 Knock over
47 Writes without pen or pencil
50 Keys
51 Don who pitched a perfect game in the 1956 World Series
54 Lollobrigida and others
55 Tip for a calligrapher
56 Dandy
58 President who won by one electoral vote
59 Space shuttle supply
61 Locale for a vision of the Apostle Paul
64 Sicken
66 Candy treat
67 Basic infirmities
70 Cousin of a credit union
71 Friendly
74 Dimensions and tolerances, say
75 Taste
78 Tot minder
79 Major player in the movie biz?
81 Certain parallel: Abbr.
82 Some Sony computers
83 Apple product
85 Proclaims
88 Extends
89 The whole song and dance?
90 1999 "Star Wars" release
92 Subject of Cyrus the Great
93 Registers
96 Nickelodeon explorer
97 Fuss
98 Fairy queen, in Shakespeare
101 Underwriter's assessment
102 It's typically off base
103 Bottom line
106 Bistro adjunct
109 Round top
111 Long of "Boyz N the Hood"
112 Cease pleading
113 Building support
116 No matter what
119 Bruised
120 Nursery rhyme dish
121 "___ I!"
122 Theodore of "The Defiant Ones"
123 Subject of una sinfonia
124 Prosperity

DOWN

1 "You're doing it all wrong!"
2 Cream-filled pastry
3 Doctor
4 Music category
5 Calculate, as the bill
6 Kind of yoga
7 Parseghian of Notre Dame
8 Without thinking
9 First two
10 Old "Romper Room" character with bouncing antennae
11 Actor McGregor
12 Newswoman Compton
13 Game with orcs and half-elves
14 Like the labyrinth of Knossos
15 Graded materials
16 Suit to ___
17 Financial inits.
18 Japanese electronics giant
19 Sack materials
21 Was overly nice
27 Choice at a restaurant
30 Unfinished threat
31 Breathe
33 Cause of a red face
34 German port
38 E Street Band's leader, informally
39 Ones with incendiary ideas
40 Simple
41 Equal alternative
42 Beyond understanding
43 Neither hor. nor vert.
45 Barker's attention-getter
47 Legend in one's own mind
48 Sign at a store clothing bin
49 Imminently
50 One way to take it
52 Contented responses
53 Arctic explorer John
57 Go for the gold?
60 Snare
62 Store chain since 1859
63 Part of a bee
65 ___ Enterprise
68 Year in the reign of Antoninus Pius
69 Like Longfellow's Evangeline
72 King's longtime home
73 Assent
76 Photographer Richard
77 Locks in a stable
80 Hi-___
84 Part of a conference sched.
86 Fishing gear
87 Have great affection for
88 Punches a new number in
91 Commercial ending with Water
92 English royal known as the Empress Maud
94 "Cooks who know trust" this, in an old slogan
95 Tourist info spot
98 TV title role for Brandy Norwood
99 Beverage named for a Dutch river
100 Actress Blair
102 Idée ___ (accepted idea, in French)
104 Gird for battle, say
105 Oscar nominee for "The Insider"
106 Banned chemicals
107 1968 live folk album
108 Odious one
109 Shy
110 "The ability to describe others as they see themselves": Lincoln
114 Offerer of cozy accommodations
115 Baseball stat
117 Election day: Abbr.
118 Musical genre

by Craig Kasper

ACROSS

1 Lays at the door of
7 One drawing sympathy
14 Tequila brand, for short
20 Any "Rock 'n' Roll High School" band member
21 Did some bookkeeping
22 Teamed up
23 Cuddly sheep?
25 Simple digs
26 TV remote, e.g.
27 Scout's find
29 Operatic prince
30 16th-century council city
31 Pen's end
33 Equinox mo.
34 Qum native
37 Eerie ability
39 Entre ___
41 Role-play, say
43 Those on the bench
46 Conservatives waiting in line?
50 Oater command
52 Wilhelm I ruled it
54 Pilot's vision problem
55 Idle, with "around"
57 A cabinet dept.
58 Blood: Prefix
60 Pro ___
61 Like a Miata
62 Expulsion from a court?
65 Treaty subject
68 Juilliard subj.
69 Necessitate
70 Mess up
73 Blasting aid
75 Carnaby Street types
77 Hillbillies' coif?
81 Hawkish
84 Test version
86 Biographer Leon
87 Ref. work with more than 300,000 entries
88 Be a fink
89 Lustrous fabric
91 Gave power to
93 Geom. solid
94 What van Gogh said regarding ears?
97 Reactor parts
98 Sinatra impersonator on "S.N.L."
100 Action film hero Williams
101 ___ Miguel (Azores island)
103 Cause of an intl. incident, maybe
104 Monokini's lack
106 ___ whim
108 Overshadow
112 Totally nuts
114 Taxco wrap
117 Edible spherule
119 Oscar-winning director of 2005
122 Sitting Bull being evasive?
124 Poverty-stricken
125 Downsize without layoffs
126 Timeless, in verse
127 Dedicated an ode to
128 Sonnet endings
129 Stopped arguing

DOWN

1 French port
2 Debussy opus
3 Go unhurriedly
4 State of increased quantity
5 Puts into effect
6 Shia, e.g.
7 Halloween activity
8 Clerical garment
9 Shoulder muscle, briefly
10 Vanilla-flavored treat
11 Cub leader
12 It may be found under a grate
13 Scene of a fall
14 1920's White House name
15 Kin of -kin
16 Lancelot lover
17 Calling the author of "In Cold Blood"?
18 Nix
19 Nose-wrinkler
24 Time on end
28 Makeshift swing
32 Nobelist Niels
35 Stays for another hitch
36 Really enjoyed
38 Druid, e.g.
40 In ___ (not yet born)
41 Wall Street option
42 Loses on purpose
43 Cross words
44 The munchies, for one
45 Swindle, slangily
47 2001 Sean Penn film
48 "___ chance"
49 Book size, in printing
51 Take a shot
53 Kick target
56 "Alfie" actress, 2004
59 Canton's home
63 Cereal box abbr.
64 Biddy
66 Pouty look
67 Insect-eating plant
71 Pool group
72 In ___ land
73 "The Sound of Music" name
74 Worthless African animal?
76 Genesis son
77 Novelist Binchy
78 Court plea, in brief
79 Thing to do
80 Some calculations
81 Carat divs.
82 Mrs. Theodore Roosevelt
83 New stylings
85 Rend
89 ___ Balls (Hostess brand)
90 Verne skipper
92 Chocolaty treats
95 Picks, with "for"
96 They're depressed during exams
99 Lost zip
102 Carol starter
104 Knuckle-dragger
105 Goes bonkers
107 Prince Valiant's son
109 Left on board
110 Alums do it
111 Sent, in a way
112 Journalist Sheehy
113 Ballerina Pavlova
115 History units
116 Jay Gould railroad
118 River of central Germany
120 Shoebox marking
121 Baseball Hall-of-Famer Roush
123 Polo Grounds legend

by Fred Piscop

ACROSS

1 Some people count by them
5 Potters' needs
10 Bits of Three Stooges violence
14 Instruction to a violinist
19 Overhead light?
20 Place for boats
21 Cut for a column
22 Ones undergoing transformation
23 Rock band whose first album was titled, appropriately, "High Voltage"
24 Announcer's cry at a hound race?
27 [Boo-hoo!]
29 Inconsistent
30 "___ Thou Now, O Soul" (Walt Whitman poem)
31 Jazz pianist Bill
33 Skirt feature
34 Flies, maybe
35 Minotaur's home
38 What priests on a space mission wear?
44 Pitch maker?
46 How sardines are often packed
47 Requirement for a hand, say
48 Receiver of donations
49 Take ___ (swing hard)
50 A celebrity carries one
52 Bldg. planner
53 Smart-mouthed
54 Prefix with -zoic
55 Classic Jaguar
56 Dr. Gregory of "ER"
59 Attack helicopter
61 King Frederick I's realm
63 Naps
65 Werner of "Ship of Fools," 1965
66 Mouthing off to police officers?
69 Informal head cover
72 Asylum seekers
73 Formally attired
77 Child actor discovered by Chaplin
79 Observe furtively
80 Atlanta-based health org.
81 Faux: Abbr.
82 Sheltered spot
83 They have big bills
85 Result of a slap, perhaps
86 ___ bean
87 Word with bitter or winter
88 Man ___
89 Abbott and Costello's "Here Come the ___"
92 Novelist Glyn who coined "It" as a euphemism
94 TV dog with its muzzle removed?
98 Teen problem
99 Chantilly seraph
100 "Norma Rae" director Martin
101 Consumer products giant, briefly
103 Fictional hero whose first words are "I was born in the Year 1632, in the City of York . . ."
106 Tissuelike
108 Tease
112 Marshes with libraries and opera houses?
115 Noted exile
116 Kitchen floor coverings, to a Brit
117 Fossey who did gorilla research
118 "The Wreck of the Mary ___"
119 Longtime NBC star
120 Dumb
121 Snafu
122 Turned up
123 Trails

DOWN

1 Sign of spring
2 City on the Brazos
3 ___ Towne
4 Debutante ball?
5 "Dreams From My Father" writer
6 Singer in the 1958 movie "Go, Johnny, Go!"
7 Night school subj.
8 His ___ (self-important man)
9 Stops daydreaming
10 "Hush!"
11 "Swan Lake" role
12 Terrible shame
13 Rte. parts
14 Lift
15 Habana or Cádiz
16 Grp. with lodges
17 Fall guys?
18 Horizontal thread in a fabric
25 Longtime Chicago Symphony conductor
26 Start of Kansas' motto
28 Cinematographer Nykvist
32 Common English place name ending
34 Big report
35 Surgical aid
36 Like triple plays compared to double plays
37 Aria that ends "O speranze d'amor!"
39 A, in Italy
40 Harvard student
41 ___ lit
42 Buckwheat groats
43 Drive . . . or part of a cattle drive
45 Horizontal line
51 Decree
52 Major extensions?
53 Backdrop for carolers?
56 "Wittle" toe
57 So out it's back in
58 Pasty
60 Foot specialist
62 Family history, e.g.
63 Short cuts
64 Stock market sell-off
67 "Without a doubt"
68 Word said with a hand behind one's back
69 1983 Mr. T film
70 Alley Oop's girl
71 Vagabond
74 Cyberchatting
75 Wheels for big wheels
76 Windows button
78 Crystal user
80 ___ number (ID on all stocks and registered bonds)
84 Symbol of royal power
85 Driller's deg.
88 Worthless
89 Some sunglasses
90 Many a John Ford film
91 Spanish road
93 Curtsier
95 City where the Lehigh and Delaware rivers meet
96 Soap operas, e.g.
97 Ones at the feeding trough
102 "Long time ___!"
103 Third-century year
104 Archaeological site
105 Bone that means "elbow" in Latin
106 Balletic bend
107 River of Flanders
109 Guess
110 Little bite
111 Doctors' grps.
113 Two-inch stripe wearer: Abbr.
114 ___ Tomé

by Paula Gamache

ACROSS

1 Pot builder
9 Solitaire measure
14 Court marshal
21 Undying flower
22 Round window
23 Condition of the 85-Across
24 Peacemaker
25 Of yore
26 Boards
27 Something that goes for a quarter?
29 How Peter denied Jesus
31 The Marx Bros. left Paramount for it
32 Subj. of a library in Austin, Tex.
35 Opposite of protruding
36 Chaise place
38 Actress Andersson of "I Never Promised You a Rose Garden"
39 Delivered a stemwinder
41 Plant sci.
43 Unification Church member, slangily
44 Loaf
45 Threw out, as a question
46 Flip out
48 "Gold" Fonda role
49 Like Van Buren's presidency
50 123-Across or 96-Down?
53 It may be polar
54 Israeli political leader Peretz
56 Original finish?
57 Howe in the National Inventors Hall of Fame
58 Diana on the cover of "Sgt. Pepper's Lonely Hearts Club Band"
59 Snowboard alternative
61 Seize
62 Quadrille designs
64 Box ofc. buy
67 127-Across or 91-Down?
70 God who cuckolded Hephaestus
71 Seating areas
72 Cause of an explosion
73 Doofus
74 Put (down)
75 Old five-franc pieces
76 23-Across or 19-Down?
83 Not camera-ready?
84 1994 film with the tagline "Get ready for rush hour"
85 Really big
86 Bows
87 Wasn't straight
88 Macon's river
89 NNW's reverse
90 Big Southern department store chain
91 "The Trouble With Harry" co-star Edmund
93 24-Across or 5-Down?
97 Once across the Rio Grande?
98 Hamburger shack?
99 Caravaggio's "The Sacrifice of ___"
100 Neptune's closest moon
103 French textile city
104 Oxford lengths
106 Norse war god
107 Saloon habitués, slangily
108 Boarders board it
109 Bordeaux wine
111 On ___ (raging)
113 Wing
114 Tail
115 Like some stars
116 Reddish gem
119 Most drunken
121 Worth having
123 VX, e.g.
127 Secondary competitions, in some tennis tournaments
128 Piano's counterpart
129 Words before roof or flag
130 Tabasco and others
131 Let out
132 Course option

DOWN

1 Rude character
2 U.K. record label
3 Dorm leaders, for short
4 Smell ___
5 Wedded couples
6 Not forgotten
7 Flute parts
8 ___ Problem of celestial mechanics
9 Codger
10 Some toll units
11 Reverse mantra of "The Shining"
12 Salt agreement?
13 Circus props
14 "Don't fight"
15 It begins here
16 About
17 J.F.K. alternative
18 "Assuming it's O.K. with you . . ."
19 Impression of Count Dracula?
20 Second-largest city in Ark.
23 Cereal toppers
28 Leaf pore
30 Sharp fellow?
32 Cut (off)
33 Bud
34 "A Different World" actress
37 Candy bar fillings
38 Fake
40 Chinese bloomers
42 Person behind bars?
44 Some gowns
46 Welcome words to a hitchhiker
47 Dropped from the galleys
49 Undermine
51 Vandeweghe of the N.B.A.
52 Not final, at law
54 Strolls
55 Ancient deity mentioned 39 times in Allen Ginsberg's "How!"
58 Slam
60 Serpentine signal
61 Overcaffeinated
62 "Six Degrees of Separation" playwright
63 Comedic spiel
64 A heart often has one
65 Place to keep toys?
66 "Shame!"
68 Nobel laureate between Hesse and Eliot
69 Heads to Harvard or Georgetown, maybe
70 It often features the quadratic formula
74 ___-10
76 An Ivy, briefly
77 Outlaw Kelly
78 Make rough
79 It's blown
80 Starbucks order
81 Unadorned
82 Rink athlete, informally
84 Trig ratios
87 Seesaw, e.g.
88 Flee like mice
89 Refurbish
91 Lack of gravity
92 Cry of relief
93 Months after Tebets
94 Real downer?
95 One-eyed leader
96 Makes a special invitation?
97 City on Lake Victoria
101 Tie indicator
102 Dial-up alternative, for short
104 Fancy homes
105 Land
107 Puppeteers Bil and Cora
109 Spanish sky
110 Liking
112 Dementieva of tennis
115 Texas metropolis nickname
117 Portland college
118 Maker of the game Dart Tag
120 Transfer ___
122 Pro
124 Indian state
125 What goes in your nose to make noise?
126 Pommes frites accompanier

by Byron Walden

ACROSS

1 Audibly shocked
6 Bar
11 Two-seaters, maybe
19 Quaint opening for a note
20 Google's domain
22 Sailing
23 First you . . .
26 Nav. rank
27 ___ kwon do
28 Bit of athletic wear
29 . . . which . . .
34 Longevity
37 Explosion maker
38 Sound off
39 Smith Brothers competitor
41 Music box?
44 Super Mario Bros. player
45 You may put something on it at a bar
49 ___ Today (teachers' monthly)
50 High-altitude home
51 Not subject to any more changes
53 Shortly
54 Kind of help
55 Depilatory brand
56 . . . that . . .
59 Sot's woe
60 Didn't play
61 Suffix with hip
62 Mai ___
63 After a while the . . .
72 ___ soda
73 "Dream on!"
74 Spanish pronoun
75 Geom. figure
76 . . . who . . .
83 House or senate
84 Med. plans
85 Sick as ___
86 Glaswegian: Glasgow :: Loiner : ___
87 Waits
88 Foreign pen pal, maybe
89 Oil tanker cargoes
91 "Looky here!"
92 Bring in
93 Ship-to-shore transport
95 "Café-Concert" painter
97 Special
98 Additional, in commercialese
99 . . . which . . .
106 Replacing
108 "___ who?"
109 QB Grossman
110 Next time . . .
117 Aesthete
118 Trojan War hero
119 Capital nicknamed "City of Trees"
120 Back-of-book feature
121 Classic Harlem ballroom
122 Story subtitled "The Yeshiva Boy"

7 Any ship
8 Concert souvenir
9 Pained sounds
10 Glimpse
11 Classic setting for detective pulp fiction
12 Win by ___
13 "Don't take ___ seriously!"
14 Antitheft device
15 Stunk
16 Part of a windy road
17 Crack team?: Abbr.
18 Bloody 2004 thriller
21 It comes with strings attached
24 Class
25 Songwriter Washington
30 Stoop feature
31 Ancient region bordering Lydia
32 Rock singer Reznor
33 Homes on the Costa del Sol
35 Subject of a makeup exam?
36 Fishhook line
39 Tall and thin
40 On base
41 Music genre, briefly
42 End
43 Do-or-die time
46 Couldn't stand
47 Año nuevo time

48 Start of the title of many an ode
51 Party
52 Lascivious
54 Men-only
56 "2001" computer
57 Nos. on a scoreboard
58 Source of an explosion in Italy
60 French town of W.W. II
64 Lip
65 Lead character on TV's "The Pretender"
66 Plains tribe
67 Kind of lic.
68 Jupiter's counterpart
69 Belief
70 Senate staff
71 Assignation
76 Mississippi senator Cochran
77 Blend
78 Modulate
79 Internet address suffix
80 Long stretches
81 Shorten, maybe
82 "What did ___ deserve this?"
83 Beginning
87 Defeat easily
89 Handel's "___ Anthems"
90 With 101-Down, unwrinkle
92 Areas next to a great hall

94 Subjects to cross-x
96 Pitching figures
99 Roughage
100 Cautious
101 See 90-Down
102 Asking too much of someone?
103 Utah senator Hatch
104 Nadir amount
105 Dismiss
107 58-Down output
110 Capture
111 Link letters
112 Lance in law
113 Indianapolis's ___ Dome
114 "Punk'd" airer
115 Resetting setting
116 Kicker?

DOWN

1 Stock phrase
2 1977 biographical Broadway play starring Anne Bancroft
3 "Ditto"
4 [as is]
5 Make-believe
6 "I Love Lucy" neighbor

by Brendan Emmett Quigley

ACROSS

1 Student's declaration
6 Restricted part of a street
13 Paul of pet food
17 1947 crime drama
21 Block in the Southwest
22 Golf club with a nearly vertical face
23 Love letters?
24 U.S. city in sight of two volcanoes
25 With 36-Across, "Poetry is . . ." (Osbert Sitwell)
27 Orange/yellow blooms
29 Feature of the villain in "The Fugitive"
30 Walk to the door
32 Single thread
33 Radisson alternative
36 See 25-Across
40 Hearty drink
43 Like the Uzbek and Kirghiz languages
47 Smog-watching grp.
48 Bagnell Dam river
49 Purplish
52 Ella of "Phantom Lady"
54 One way to be paid
58 Amount past due?
59 "Poetry is . . ." (Joseph Roux)
63 Oater locale
64 Where Springsteen was born, in song
65 Monte ___
66 Hyde Park stroller
68 Toil
71 Have on
75 Japanese band?
78 Like many pubs
81 With 89-Across, "Poetry is . . ." (Carl Sandburg)
85 Flat
88 Struggle
89 See 81-Across
93 QB Rodney
94 Banned spray
95 Russian city or oblast
96 Office gizmo
98 Soissons seasons
100 Baseball Hall-of-Famer Banks
104 Make an inauguration affirmation
107 Literary ending
111 "Poetry is . . ." (Edith Sitwell)
117 Took top honors
118 French city in W.W. II fighting
119 Title character in a "Sgt. Pepper" song
120 Grant maker
121 Hatch from Utah
123 15 years before the Battle of Hastings
125 Dead Sea Scrolls scribe
127 "___ gratias"
128 "Poetry is . . ." (Pablo Neruda)
133 Verges on
136 Sing "Gladly the cross-eyed bear," say
137 Tyro
141 ___ Mae
145 Elderly
148 "Poetry is . . ." (E. E. Cummings)
151 English university V.I.P.s
152 Punjabi believer
153 No more
154 #24 of 24
155 As a result
156 Besides
157 Fall field worker
158 Snooped (around)

DOWN

1 Bueno's opposite
2 Tennis edge
3 It may start with someone entering a bar
4 West Indian sorcery
5 Prepare, as a side of beans
6 Beantown, on scoreboards
7 Durham sch.
8 Half of doce
9 Energy
10 Singer India. ___
11 ___ this world
12 Nutrition drink brand
13 Belief
14 Up to one's ears (in)
15 Cuban patriot José
16 Go around
17 Beachwear
18 "Zounds," e.g.
19 Antiquity, quaintly
20 Denials
26 "This is where ___"
28 Alternative fuel
31 Halfhearted
34 Go bad
35 Red hair, e.g.
37 Arabian capital
38 Fairy-tale menace
39 G.P.A. spoilers
40 Mtn. stats
41 Trevi coin, once
42 Month after Ab
44 Friends
45 Not on the border
46 Poetic break: Var.
50 Sitting on
51 Tapas bar offering
53 Writer Sontag
55 Big spinner
56 Here, in Juárez
57 Camera inits.
60 Aligned
61 Main seating area
62 Namely
67 Perfect
69 N.C. State plays in it
70 Denny's alternative
72 Oklahoma city
73 Steinbeck's "To ___ Unknown"
74 Angry talk
75 Really, really
76 Physicist Niels
77 "Dies ___"
79 Arrived quietly
80 ". . . ___ great fall"
82 Exactly, after "to"
83 Parlor piece
84 Gridiron protection
86 Wasted gas
87 Inventor's place
90 Group of spies
91 Kind of check
92 Hundred Acre Wood donkey
97 Winter Olympics venues
99 It's raised on a farm
101 NASA homecoming
102 Tiny bite
103 "See ___ care!"
105 Two, in Lisbon
106 In many cases
108 Operatic Jenny
109 Early Nebraskan
110 Deli order
111 Old deferment classification
112 Beeper
113 Ticking off
114 Pulled in
115 Poe's middle name
116 Surrealist Magritte
122 Reply to "No way!"
124 Old-style hangover remedy
126 League division
129 Mighty big
130 Swing wildly
131 Corner office and others
132 Gettysburg general under Lee
134 Household health hazard
135 Sportscast feature
138 Peevishness
139 TV's Swenson
140 Fashion's ___ von Furstenberg
142 "Here ___ . . ."
143 "Bus Stop" playwright
144 "Yikes!"
145 "___ on Melancholy"
146 Swe. abutter
147 Ma'am or dam
149 K.C.-to-Duluth dir.
150 "___ the fields . . ."

by Victor Fleming

ACROSS

1 Rude awakening
5 Frequent abbr. on sheet music for folk songs
9 Compound number?
14 Without an out
19 1998 Andrea Bocelli operatic album
20 DeSoto or LaSalle
21 Concentration thwarter
22 Something that might be tucked under the chin
23 . . . and 25-Across have "canine" surnames
25 . . . and 41-Across sang with their siblings
27 Ignore the alarm
28 "With any luck"
30 Shamed
31 Save one's own neck, maybe
32 Poet with a seemingly self-contradictory name
33 Bundle of nerves
34 Barely perceptible
36 Reach a settlement
37 Healing aid patented in 1872
41 . . . and 52-Across are Mormons
43 Matches
44 No Westminster contender
45 Compass point suffix
46 Not at all certain
47 Contest that leads to a draw
48 Loyal pooch
49 Census stats
51 Agassi partner
52 . . . and 69-Across have affiliations with "Jeopardy!"
55 Museum employee
57 The King of Pop, in headlines
58 1980s–'90s N.B.A. star Danny
59 Belligerent deity
60 Branches
61 He reached his peak in 1806
62 "Everybody Loves Raymond" role
64 News exec Roger
65 Glockenspiels' kin
69 . . . and 80-Across have mythological creatures as surnames
71 Mmes., across the Pyrenees
72 Symbol in el zodiaco
73 "Zip-___-Doo-Dah"
74 Have an in (with)
75 Stimulate
76 Kia model
77 "Didn't I tell you?!"
78 Faith in music
80 . . . and 99-Across starred in musicals and share their first names with a classic sitcom couple
84 Comment following a lucky guess
86 Pin site
87 Slippery as ___
88 Taking care of the situation
89 France's Oscar
90 "The Most Happy Fella" song
91 Bailiwick of TV's Matlock
94 Country with a palm tree on its flag
95 Sophocles subject
99 . . . and 101-Across are known for their fancy footwork

101 . . . and 23-Across are Olympic gold medalists
103 Clan symbol
104 Makes
105 Xena's horse
106 Absence
107 Talked a blue streak?
108 Showed courage, old-style
109 In case
110 Caustic chemicals

DOWN

1 Fixes
2 Exam format
3 Erstwhile denaro
4 Cons
5 Access
6 Contrite
7 Long-distance letters
8 Exhibiting ennui
9 Had fun with
10 Rogaine alternative
11 Cheryl of "Curb Your Enthusiasm"
12 Tongue's end?
13 Not totally disastrous
14 Flies
15 Strands in the winter?
16 This and that
17 Sheltered
18 Sale locale
24 Like hedgehogs
26 Bigger than big
29 Keratoid
34 Make a name for oneself?
35 Queen ___ County, Md.
36 Elizabeth Taylor's pet charity, for short
37 Mission ___, Calif.
38 Hockey infraction
39 Wink accompaniment
40 Asteroid discovered in 1898
41 Pricey
42 Donkeys, to mules
43 Discards
47 Casino supply
48 Police epithet, with "the"
50 Make fast
51 "The Female Eunuch" author
52 Singer/actress Akers
53 Performs perfectly
54 Puma rival
56 Before markdown: Abbr.
57 Half of Brangelina
60 Grant money?
61 Masterpiece
62 Jilted wife of myth
63 Staggering
64 "Is that ___?"
65 Truculent
66 Leader of the Mel-Tones
67 Typeface akin to Helvetica
68 Expeditiously
69 Like il but not elle: Abbr.
70 Sore
71 Round all around
75 March honoree, familiarly
78 George Eliot, e.g.
79 Uses a Moviola, in film-making
80 Showing the least resistance
81 Close-fitting garment
82 Georgia of "The Mary Tyler Moore Show"
83 Erythrocyte
85 U.P.S. staffer, at times
86 Memorizes
89 Cicada sound
90 Baffin Bay sights
91 P.M. periods
92 Think way back?
93 Actor Jared
96 Bob of the P.G.A.
97 It may be served in a bed
98 Shows curiosity
100 Sports org. for nonprofessionals
102 "Chances ___"

by Henry Hook

ACROSS

1 Tribe with a sun dance
6 Periods in contrast to global warming
13 Cuff
17 Rise and fall, as a ship
18 Team supporter's suction cup–mounted sign
19 Regardful
20 Where smart shoppers shop?
23 Ad ___
24 Lodges
25 Fake-out
26 Short-order cook's aid
27 A person doing a duck walk grasps these
29 Site of Napoleon's invasion of 1798–1801
31 Place for fish and ships
32 Tell
33 "___ me!"
34 Plight of an overcrowded orchestra?
38 Cat, at times
40 Computer file name extension
41 Camera inits.
42 Kind of sch.
43 Crew
46 Fit for dwelling
51 Blushing
52 Introduction to opera?
54 Epitome of blackness
55 Oodles
57 Frustrated
58 Gaynor of "South Pacific"
59 Common origami creations
61 Sought sanctuary, old-style
63 ___ "Inferno"
64 Lilylike plant
65 Actress Shire and others
66 Insider talk
67 Not exceeding
68 Locale of Hoosier beaches?
71 Bub
74 Leaving, slangily
76 Virus variety
77 "Essays of ___"
78 Bow
79 "___ now!"
81 Yes-men, maybe?
83 Bit of winter exercise?
89 Italian librettist Gaetano ___
90 Abbr. after many a military title
91 Match
92 Annual announcement from 13-Down
93 "Drink to me only with thine eyes" poet
94 Burmese gathering?
97 "Ciao"
98 Carolina university
100 Dog with a tightly curled tail
101 Geraldo rehearses his show?
105 Much-counterfeited timepiece
106 More run-down
107 Traction provider
108 ___ empty stomach
109 Mugs
110 Hopper of Hollywood

DOWN

1 Dish for an Italian racing champ?
2 Stimpy's TV pal
3 Most like a breeze
4 Dame Edith who was nominated for three Oscars
5 In stitches
6 "___ tree falls . . ."
7 Stephen King's first novel
8 Last
9 "Far out!"
10 Show fixation, maybe
11 Stowe girl
12 Composer Prokofiev
13 See 92-Across: Abbr.
14 French Bluebeard
15 Cultural/teaching facility
16 Una ___ (old coin words)
19 Calais confidant
20 Item on a chain, usually
21 Steers clear of
22 Passage
23 Nautical rope
28 Former Irish P.M. ___ Cosgrave
30 Québec traffic sign
31 Stole
34 ___ hammer (Viking symbol)
35 Show slight relief, maybe
36 Computer key
37 Kind of paper
39 Whoops
44 Basket material
45 Iowa and Missouri
47 A club, e.g.
48 Sandwich that can never be finished?
49 Be a couch potato
50 "___ Coming" (1969 hit)
52 Tiny annoyance
53 Gouges repeatedly
56 Overall
58 Jazz's Herbie
59 Thick-bodied fish
60 Cowboy's aid
61 Send out
62 Denver's ___ Gardens amusement park
63 Photographer Arbus
65 "Star Trek: ___"
66 German camera
68 Canine neighbor
69 Words often applied to 93-Across
70 Hen, at times
72 Freshens
73 Cover
75 Bug
77 School named in the Public Schools Act of 1868
80 Many urban dwellers
82 Like electrical plugs
83 Hall of Fame jockey Eddie
84 Become tiresome to
85 Loser at the Battle of Châlons, A.D. 451
86 Birthplace of Aaron Burr
87 "Happy Days" role
88 Lessener
93 Eponymous physicist
95 1932 skiing gold medalist Utterström
96 Bit of spelling?
97 King ___ tomp
99 ___ Lomond
102 Historic Heyerdahl craft
103 Prof.'s posting
104 Fooled

by Charles M. Deber

ACROSS

1 Like windows and geishas
7 Subject of a David McCullough political biography
12 Copper head?
15 Staying power
19 Chevy introduced in 1958
20 Time's 1977 Man of the Year
21 Strong draft horses
23 *What someone who looks at Medusa does
25 Act of putting into circulation
26 Private line
27 "___-La-La" (Al Green hit)
28 "A Lonely Rage" autobiographer
30 "Star Trek" series, to fans
31 Laws, informally
32 *1850 American literature classic
37 From ___ Z
39 Suffix with convention
40 Faulkner hero
41 Shakespearean question after "How now!"
42 *Demonstrate the method
48 Staying power?
50 Bus. card abbr.
51 Your highness?: Abbr.
52 ___-mo
53 Stuffs
54 Area of authority
56 It has gutters on each side
59 "The Lord of the Rings" creature
61 Mary of "Where Eagles Dare"
62 Cost of time or space
63 Without a break
65 Succeed
69 Agnus ___ (Mass prayers)
70 *Push aside
73 TV's "___-Team"
75 Meets, as a challenge
78 Kind of patch
79 Received, as a message
80 Eydie Gormé's "___ Es el Amor"
81 Hair-raising cry
84 Boxer Trinidad
85 Becker on "L.A. Law"
86 Verve
88 Run down
90 ___ 88
92 State with the fewest counties (three): Abbr.
93 John who hosted TV's "Talk Soup"
94 *Walk in the park, say
98 "Wouldn't ___ Loverly?"
99 House calls?
101 Battery size
102 High-school dept.
103 *Put at bay
108 Appointees confirmed by Cong.
112 Did not go fast?
113 Film noir, e.g.
114 ___ Schwarz
115 "Well, look ___!"
116 "Hamlet" setting
119 *Miami baseball list
122 British composer Robert
123 Have ___ in mind
124 Gertrude who swam the English Channel
125 Not included: Abbr.
126 9-1-1 grp.
127 Percolates
128 They may be light or free

DOWN

1 Relative of a mandolin
2 Tickle
3 Cutting
4 It goes back and forth in a workshop
5 Further
6 "Gimme ___!"
7 "Steady ___ goes"
8 Computer input
9 Big flap
10 Victorian roofs
11 Leather source
12 McMurry University site
13 Lays siege to
14 Mass transit choices
15 *Toothless South American animal
16 Seemed right
17 Money rival
18 Bisected fly?
22 "___ Nacht" (German words of parting)
24 Kyrgyzstan city
29 Support group
32 Diligent student, in slang
33 These: Fr.
34 Eases off
35 Head set
36 MapQuest request: Abbr.
38 English class assignment
42 Pricey strings
43 Attentive one
44 Sainted king called "the Stout"
45 Defeatees' comment
46 Son of Cedric the Saxon
47 Word of encouragement
49 Banjo-picker Scruggs
55 *Not so important
57 Opposite of paleo-
58 P.O. item
60 Place for a star
64 Girl in a gown
66 "Misty" composer Garner
67 "___ the Magician" (old radio series)
68 More chilling
71 Table scrap
72 Sundial hour
74 Gustav Klimt's "Portrait of ___ Bloch-Bauer!"
76 Start of Idaho's motto
77 Woody's partner
79 Sets upon
82 Kinetoscope inventor
83 Mrs. Doonesbury, in the comics
86 "___ life!"
87 Fair-minded
89 Modern and technologically advanced
91 Pricey
93 Smart
94 Lush fabrics
95 ___-tzu
96 Deerstalker fold-down
97 "Boston Legal" Emmy winner
100 Memory trace
104 Oversee
105 1980s major-league slugger Tony
106 Accomplishes perfectly, as a dismount
107 Lot of time
109 Fort ___, Fla.
110 Synthetic gem
111 Film extras, for short
115 Page, for one
116 Conductor ___-Pekka Salonen
117 Old Ford
118 East End abode
120 Fish eggs
121 Pentateuch book: Abbr.

by Jim Page

MORE HEADLINES THAT MAKE YOU GO "HUH?"

ACROSS

1 Trick-taking card game
5 Yemeni port famous as a source of coffee
10 Former Connecticut governor Ella
16 Take in
21 Swenson of "Benson"
22 Saw
23 Comparatively flush
24 "No men allowed" area
25 Ambiguous headline about a man charged with killing his attacker?
29 Mystic
30 Level of care
31 Connected, in a way
32 Bright-eyed
35 Santa ___
36 Earth Day subj.
38 Retired boomer
39 Ambiguous headline about a protest?
48 Gone by
49 Parcel
50 Company with the slogan "born from jets"
51 Field protector
52 Sandwich rank
54 Take ___ breath
56 Hang over
59 "What ___?"
63 Ambiguous headline about school closings?
69 Oil-rich ruler
70 Dutch painter Jan
71 Hair-raiser
72 Fall setting
73 Was contrite
76 Break
78 Field stars
80 Early hrs.
81 Ambiguous headline about a California drug bust?
87 Rocky peak
88 One with a thick skin
89 ". . . ___ saw Elba"
90 Actress Sedgwick
91 JFK-to-TLV option
93 Peter and Paul, but not Mary
95 Sugar cube holder
98 Rating of a program blocked by a V-chip
101 Ambiguous headline about a vagrancy statistic?
106 Moonshine
107 Progress smoothly
108 Broom ___ (comics witch)
109 "___ & Stitch," 2002 animated film
111 Encouraging sounds
114 Cozy corner
117 Country singer Carter
119 McKellen of "The Lord of the Rings"
120 Ambiguous headline about attorneys' pro bono work?
125 Do-do connector
127 Jump in the rink
128 "___ of Destruction," 1965 protest song
129 Actor Morales
130 Words said with raised arm and glass
133 Word for word
138 Huge
142 Ambiguous headline about a stolen Stradivarius?
146 Kind of chin
147 Vast
148 Heavy metal bar
149 Like the rim of an eyecup
150 Earthenware pots
151 Kind of valve
152 Wild guesses
153 It's not held when it's used

DOWN

1 Sets (on)
2 In the ___
3 It'll douse a fuego
4 Frequent congestion site
5 "Welcome" offerer
6 Kitchen gadget company
7 Big name in credit cards
8 Blast maker
9 "The Bonesetter's Daughter" author
10 1983 U.S. invasion site
11 Narrow inlets
12 Dramatic opening
13 Quake
14 One of New York's Finger Lakes
15 E-mail address ender
16 Place for a guard, in soccer
17 Shaker formula
18 Word with scam or sketch
19 Means of control
20 Irish patriot hanged in 1803
26 Close
27 Elaine ___ ("Seinfeld" role)
28 One end of the Moscow Canal
33 Longtime staple of daytime TV
34 Popular air freshener
37 Dated
39 West of Hollywood
40 Playing marble
41 Composer Ned
42 Their service is impeccable
43 Mushroom cloud creator, briefly
44 Columbo portrayer
45 Duo in a typical symphony
46 Exhort
47 Sudden increase on a graph
53 Scottish estate owner
55 Prefix with dactyl
57 Muppet who lives in a trash can
58 Mazda model
60 "Myra Breckinridge" novelist
61 Abnormal plant swelling
62 Info that may be phished: Abbr.
64 Trounce
65 "Still Me" autobiographer Christopher
66 Some magazine ads
67 Schlock
68 In need of a washer, perhaps
74 Head of costume design
75 Lush
77 Palm readers?
79 Gaiety
81 Manuscript sheet
82 Muse with a wreath of myrtle and roses
83 Makes unwanted overtures?
84 Jazz pianist Chick
85 Breeze
86 Maritime
87 High-___
92 Sock fiber
94 Definitely no arm-twister
96 Father Sarducci of old "S.N.L."
97 Fifth-century pope
99 11th-century year
100 Company with a "spokesduck"
102 Newsman Bernard
103 "The Time Machine" race
104 "Do ___?"
105 Grannies
110 It's next to nothing
112 "Grand" hotel
113 Reason for a 98-Across
115 Not neat
116 N.F.L. running back Barlow
118 Rhett Butler's last words
120 Choo-choo name
121 Trust
122 Most cunning
123 Hip locale
124 MTV's owner
125 Transmission repair franchise
126 Silver quarters?
131 Film brand
132 Numismatists' goals
134 Author Janowitz
135 Composer Satie
136 It might get the brush-off
137 Home stretches?
139 Joe
140 Anthem starter
141 Move, in Realtor lingo
143 Poli ___
144 High ball?
145 "___ true"

by Seth A. Abel

ACROSS

1 Lhasa ___
5 Breathing tube
12 Old cracker brand
16 Back on board
19 Pfizer product used before brushing the teeth
20 Anne who wrote "Abie's Irish Rose"
21 Reason to shout "Eureka!"
22 Language along the Mekong River
23 Play about tenderizing meat with one's toes?
26 Beast with a bugling call
27 Patronize, as a hotel
28 "Let's Make a Deal" choice
29 Red spot on the skin
31 Musical drama about a butcher who sells deer meat?
37 ___ de Cologne
38 Honoree's spot
39 Gullets
40 Musical play set at McDonald's?
49 Dangerous place to pass a car
50 Pole, e.g.
51 Even
52 Actress Barbara Bel ___
54 In love
55 Blast
56 Windsor princess
58 Muppets' creator
59 Musical drama that tells the tale of a sausage casing?
61 Hat trick component
63 Ring holder
64 Musical drama about a man eating soup?
72 Mulling spice
78 Many baseball card stats
79 What you may call it
80 Business with net gains?
81 Tighten, say, as strings
82 1962 hit film whose climax is on Crab Key island
83 Conveys
84 Place in the pecking order
85 Play about a guy ordering beef from Dublin?
88 Martini & Rossi offering
89 Little fellow
90 Despite this
91 Play about swine intestines that are semidivine?
101 Miner's major problem
102 White sheet
103 Person who has something going on?
105 Allen Ginsberg's "Plutonian ___"
106 Play about meat that's good to eat anytime?
112 Elbow-bender
113 Brand name with an accent on its last letter
114 Character in many a joke
115 B.A. or M.A. offerer
116 Retired number of Dodger Tommy Lasorda
117 Goblet part
118 Juvenal work
119 Pageantry

DOWN

1 "Be on the lookout" messages, briefly
2 Oliver of "The West Wing"
3 "The Terminator" heroine
4 Common daisy
5 U.S. bond market purchase
6 Kia subcompact
7 Stage entertainment
8 N.L. and A.L. city
9 Passport maker
10 Mr. ___, scheming vicar in "Emma"
11 Take ___ at
12 Stylin'
13 Swearing-in phrase
14 Deity credited with inventing the lyre
15 Like Hoosier cabinets
16 Composer Scarlatti
17 Popular quarry for British hunters
18 Arcade game inserts
24 Relations: Abbr.
25 Worn away
30 Meant to attract
32 Possessed girl in "The Exorcist"
33 Town largely destroyed by the Battle of Normandy
34 "Ben-___"
35 Quite a ways
36 Using
40 Radio host John
41 "Dialogues Concerning Natural Religion" author
42 The Isle of Man's Port ___
43 Nonhuman co-hosts of TV's "Mystery Science Theater 3000"
44 Incumbent on
45 Attack once more
46 Sky light
47 Palette globs
48 Trapper's prize
49 Does a certain dog trick
52 Sickly-looking
53 Slovenly abode
55 Thermometer's terminus
56 Get stuck
57 Drink suffix
59 Fistfuls, say
60 Phaser setting
62 Missing broadcast channel
64 Scorecard heading
65 Dwarf
66 Compared with
67 Symbol of hardness
68 Talk, talk, talk: Var.
69 Memo header
70 Steinway & ___ (piano maker)
71 What, to Watteau
73 Five-Year Plan implementer, for short
74 "The Cosby Show" kid
75 Badlands landform
76 Bow-wielding deity
77 "Peer ___"
80 Diets drastically
82 Go from endangered to extinct
83 Slapstick missiles
85 First name in Objectivism
86 Bibliophile's love: Abbr.
87 Grain susceptible to ergot
88 Buttonhole
89 W.W. I helmet, informally
92 Inventive sorts?
93 Line at the dentist's office?
94 Main line
95 Sprung
96 Some mantel pieces
97 Mens ___
98 Get fuel
99 University of Maine's home
100 Shade of blue
104 Get back to
107 Gray
108 Closemouthed
109 Hula dancer's accessory
110 Common pg. size
111 "Didn't I tell you?"

by Patrick Berry

JOB DESCRIPTIONS

ACROSS

1 Key of Beethoven's "Für Elise"
7 Some trigonometric ratios
14 Sarcastic comment of sympathy
20 "Dr. Strangelove," e.g.
21 Parsnip, e.g.
22 Bewitched
23 Charles Schwab?
25 Service group
26 Cows
27 Vehicle on 30-Across
29 "This means business" look
30 See 27-Across
31 Annie Oakley?
34 Title girl in a 1962 Roy Orbison hit
37 ___ voce (quietly)
40 Others, to Pedro
41 Assimilate
44 Southwest chips-and-chili snacks
46 Viking landing site
50 Leonardo da Vinci?
52 Like one end of a battery terminal
54 "We the Living" author Rand
55 Equine
56 It has five pillars
60 Saffron's mom on "Ab Fab"
61 "My dear lady"
62 Place that's all abuzz
63 Sordid
64 Sigmund Freud?
69 Tiger Woods?
71 Rectify
72 Dish eaten with chopsticks
74 "___ would seem"
75 George Bush or Dick Cheney, once
76 Continental boundary
77 Easter Island is a province of it
79 It needs refining
82 Author/journalist Fallaci
84 Benjamin Franklin?
87 Illustrations: Abbr.
88 Cutting humor
92 "Lord Jim" star, 1965
93 Disney subsidiary
94 Gleans
96 Contemptuous expression
97 Bill Gates?
102 Seed cover
105 Cartoon mermaid
106 Construction company
107 Just make out
112 Bedtime for junior, maybe
114 Babe Ruth?
117 Country singer West
118 Nutty
119 Stranded by winter weather, perhaps
120 Initial stages
121 Sees about
122 Zeus' domain, in myth

DOWN

1 Second: Abbr.
2 SAT section
3 "Like ___ not . . ."
4 Court encouragement
5 Like Mork of "Mork & Mindy"
6 Front of a manuscript leaf
7 Smith who won the 1972 Wimbledon
8 Stirrup sites
9 Cruncher of nos.
10 Pendulum's path
11 Wrong
12 Skater's leap
13 Overlapping fugue motifs
14 See or call
15 Where hens sit
16 Grad school grillings
17 Starts in on
18 "Idomeneo," e.g.
19 Ursine : bear :: lutrine : ___
24 Chops
28 Awful
31 Mix up
32 Tout's offering
33 Pioneer org.
34 Eastern title
35 Silent auction site
36 Part of N.A.A.C.P.: Abbr.
38 Wastes
39 TV dinner holder
42 Set after melting
43 Panoramic
45 Legendary Gaelic poet
46 Classic flivver
47 Something to bid
48 Billboard chart category
49 Leaves rolling in the aisles
51 Faux gold
53 Agnostic
57 Ontario or Supérieur
58 "Chances ___"
59 Common muscle protein
61 Pokémon and the Beatles, once
62 Nutritionist Davis
64 ___ the dinosaur (extinction)
65 Japanese porcelain
66 1983 Woody Allen mockumentary
67 Backing
68 The Monkees' "___ Believer"
70 Shakespearean compilation
73 San ___, Argentina
77 Pet plant
78 Web address lead-in
79 Radio letter between Nan and Peter
80 Three strikes and you're out, e.g.
81 Hungarian spa town
83 "This won't hurt ___"
85 Tony-winning actress Verdon
86 "Leave it to Beaver" catchphrase
89 Skater's leap
90 Welsh cheese dish
91 Army outfit
93 Sermon site
95 Cutty ___ (clipper ship)
97 "No prob!"
98 Rigel's constellation
99 Breath fresheners
100 Quarterback Rodney
101 ___ Quinn, formerly of "S.N.L."
103 Make like new
104 Tchaikovsky's middle name
107 Tempt
108 Bowed, to a violist
109 Root beer feature
110 Estrada of "CHiPs"
111 Start of a counting-out rhyme
113 Enero, e.g.
115 Former name for Ben-Gurion Airport
116 N, E, S and W

by Kelsey Blakley

ACROSS

1 Cause for a massage
5 K.G.B. predecessor
9 Crookspeak
14 Blog comments
19 Crony
20 Look
21 Risibility
22 Poet who wrote "Immature poets imitate; mature poets steal"
23 Tax relief, e.g.
26 Churchillian trademark
27 Chapter
28 Lies
29 Subject of a Boito opera
31 "Down ___" (Janis Joplin song)
32 Be too tight
34 Doc's wife in "Come Back, Little Sheba"
35 Timeline breaks
37 December laughs
38 "___ the morning!"
39 Mary Shelley subtitle, with "The"
44 Moved purposefully
46 Windsurfers' mecca
47 Using one's shirtsleeve as a napkin, e.g.
48 Big letter
52 Free, in a way
55 "Fish Magic" and "Twittering Machine"
56 Fig. in TV's "Third Watch"
58 TV star who directed the 1999 documentary "Barenaked in America"
61 Thingumbob
63 Consume piggishly
64 Piggy
65 Lhasa ___
69 "The End of the Affair" author, 1951
71 Miracle-___
72 "___ Crazy" (1977 Paul Davis hit)
74 Car body strengtheners
76 Answers, for short
77 Sot spot
79 Stately old dance
82 Father of Henry II
83 Fall event, usually
87 Doc bloc: Abbr.
88 Palatable
91 Live in the past?
92 World's biggest city built on continuous permafrost
94 Priority system
96 Short notes
98 Branch of Islam
101 Matter of W.W. II secrecy
107 Mindful of
108 Special ___
109 Rank and file
110 Dudley Do-Right's love
111 Permanently
112 CAT scan units
114 Cheese ___
116 Transverse rafter-joining timber
118 Reading and others: Abbr.
119 Comment made while crossing the fingers
121 Serigraph
124 Skyscraper
125 Batch of Brownies
126 Back then, back when
127 Bleu hue
128 ___ cards (ESP testers)
129 They're the pits
130 Short ways to go?
131 "The Mysterious Island" captain

DOWN

1 Countenances
2 Early racer
3 Contortionist
4 Ottoman, e.g.: Abbr.
5 Jump over
6 "Just a ___" (Marlene Dietrich's last film)
7 1914 Booth Tarkington novel
8 Disentangle
9 "Under the Pink" singer Tori
10 Circular edge
11 Put on a happy face
12 Lake that James Fenimore Cooper called Glimmerglass
13 First sign
14 Lifter's rippler
15 Salmagundi
16 Words of endorsement
17 Robert Burns poem
18 Italicizes, e.g.
24 Burning issue
25 Give up on détente
30 Barrel org.
33 It's for the birds
36 Stir up
39 Broad terrace with a steep side
40 World's smallest island nation
41 Castigatory
42 Fully ready
43 Flag raiser
45 Côte d'Or's capital
49 Chinese philosopher Chuang-___
50 Nonmechanized weapon
51 Boeing worker: Abbr.
53 European Union member since 2004
54 Car that "beats the gassers and the rail jobs" in a 1964 hit
56 Adam and Eve, at a diner
57 "Harlequin's Carnival" painter
59 Initial sounds of a relief effort?
60 Good name for a minimalist?
62 Handel oratorio
66 Russian literary award established in 1881
67 Glass bottom
68 Where the Storting sits
70 energystar.gov grp.
73 Slightly tainted
75 Bridge supports
78 Alternative to the euro: Abbr.
80 Pianist Rubinstein
81 Hair-raising cry
84 Mystery award
85 Kurt denial?
86 Sign of neglect
88 Swiss resort with the Cresta Run
89 Ally of the Cheyenne
90 Gets to commit
93 Capital of Valais canton
95 Where Huxley taught Orwell
97 Kind of barrier
99 It sticks to the ribs
100 The whale in "Pinocchio"
102 New wrinkles
103 Reach for the stars
104 Vocal opponent
105 Second-highest mountain in the lower 48 states
106 Q player in "Die Another Day"
111 Devilkin
113 Admiral who went down with the Scharnhorst
115 ___-eyed
116 Recipe measures: Abbr.
117 Social workers
120 Muff
122 Sent sprawling
123 Turned yellow, maybe

by Bob Klahn

ACROSS

1 Smears
7 Fells
11 Looks for help
15 1954 sci-fi movie with an exclamation point in its title
19 Arctic wear
20 "Il mio tesoro," e.g.
21 1980s fad item
22 Blood: Prefix
23 Yosemite Sam's cursing of Bugs Bunny's food?
25 That's a lot to do
27 Then preceder
28 Explanation for why some pillows do weird things?
30 Domingo, e.g.
31 Wash (out)
33 Photo lab abbr.
34 "Stupid," in Spanish(!)
35 Armpit, to a doctor
37 Oscar winner Helen
39 Psychiatrist's scheduling
41 Theological schools: Abbr.
43 Part of baking powder
46 Letters from Atlanta
47 Basic food choice?
55 Noontime service
56 Handi-Wrap alternative
57 Flavor tasted in some wine
58 Frees
62 [Knock], in poker
64 Mile-high world capital
66 Be the 4 in a 5-4 decision
67 Natl. Safe Toys and Gifts Mo.
68 Short-term worker who causes utter disaster?
73 Jackie's "O"
74 They're beside sides
76 Boat propeller
77 Singer K. T. ___
79 Walnut and others
80 Kind of tape
83 "Livin' on ___ time" (lyric in a #1 Don Williams country hit)
85 Lineman's datum
86 Jazz-loving young entomologist?
90 Bon ___
93 Imp
94 Slew
95 Precipitately
98 Artificial, in a way
102 Has-been
106 Puffball seed
107 Draft pick?
109 Puts up
111 ___ nuevo
112 Meal for the Three Little Pigs?
116 Lola, e.g., in "Damn Yankees"
117 Intrinsically
118 Work on analytical psychology?
121 Czech composer Janácek
122 Stretched out
123 Sports Illustrated 1998 co-Sportsman of the Year
124 Brown shade
125 Sea eagle
126 Abbr. at the bottom of a business letter
127 Too-too
128 "Ready to go?"

DOWN

1 Too-too
2 Stuck
3 Stuntwork?
4 As a result
5 Varnish ingredient
6 Some Jamaican music
7 Early casino proprietor
8 Beethoven's Third
9 Occult
10 N. Dak. neighbor
11 Do something about
12 Cover for a grandmother
13 Hot spot
14 Put (away)
15 "___ Company"
16 Pleasure-filled
17 Boston college
18 "Gilligan's Island" castaway
24 Way to go: Abbr.
26 ___ law
29 Car famous for its 1950s tailfins
31 Ran
32 "Falcon Crest" co-star
36 Measurers of logical reasoning, for short
38 Ballpark fig.
39 "How ya doin'?"
40 Designer Pucci
42 Winds
44 Narc's agcy.
45 Bug
47 "P.S. I Love You" and "Revolution," e.g.
48 "Be saved!"
49 Bet to win and place
50 "Darn it all!"
51 Naïf
52 Coin word
53 ___ girl
54 Floors
59 Experimental underwater habitat
60 "Lucia di Lammermoor" baritone
61 Like Limburger cheese
63 Position that's an anagram, appropriately, of "notes"
65 Providers of cuts
66 Water seeker
69 Announcer's call after three strikes
70 Numerical prefix
71 Dance seen on TV's "Hullabaloo"
72 Hello ___, shop frequently seen on Letterman
75 Tease
78 Certain NCO's
80 1953 Wimbledon winner Seixas
81 Small chuckle
82 Ran through, as a card
84 Rearward, at sea
87 College sr.'s test
88 1980's "Double Fantasy" collaborator
89 They're encountered in "close encounters"
90 Lose in one's drawers
91 Not oral
92 James who wrote "Rule, Britannia"
96 Melodic
97 "Note to ___ . . ."
99 Portuguese Mister
100 Swiss-American composer Bloch
101 Record keeper?
103 They do dos
104 Chant
105 Ogle
107 Stuffy spot
108 Rhone's capital
110 French wine classification
113 Site of Beinecke Library
114 Digitize, maybe
115 "___ girl!"
116 Biblical brother
119 Intelligence grp.
120 Poet/musician ___ Scott-Heron

by Tony Orbach and Patrick Blindauer

Answers

Crossword Solutions

1

```
APBS  STAMP  BANCO  WISP
SHEP  LIBERTYBELL  ENTR
PONE  AMELIORATED  IDEE
INJECTED  CEN  SAMISENS
READIER  SYES  TENSPOT
ATM  ASSAI  ASSNS  EPI
TRI  UNPLUGS  NAG
EEN  PAS  REN  WER  DDE
DEFLATE  NOTSO  ICELESS
RISER  SOFTY  NOTIN
TOADS  AFROS  EPCOT
ANN  BUP  SEP  AIS  EMU
RFK  YODA  PEP  SMUT  HEB
MIL  SOG  IDA  SAP  ALE
ALIST  NOPROBLEM  ABLER
CENTE  DAIMLER  BOLTS
ED  ASTENT  DU
DAT  TOP  BIT  ESS
ACHIEVABLE  ONIONTARTS
ICANRELATE  ROSEGARDEN
STRESSMARK  OVERSLEEPS
```

2

```
BEGUMS  ESCUDOS  SAPPHO
ARARAT  PAISANO  POURED
COLADA  EDGARALLANPONY
KILLERBEANIE  IRE  TBS
ECO  AMA  TAR  TREK  BEAS
RAP  NAIL  MEAT  DEANE
CONTEMPTOFCOURTNEY
ROBOT  IDEALLY  RAH
ERASERS  XACTO  DICESUP
WITHOUTACLOONEY  LENA
ROT  FEES  ANEW  ASP
ALES  THEKARATEKIDNEY
PENPALS  XANAX  SEDUCER
ERA  PITCREW  ELENI
REMEMBERTHEALIMONY
IPODS  JOEY  TART  BUS
TIVO  LEWD  PRO  ICH  ENT
AGE  ROC  FROMONHEINIE
LOOKOUTBOLOGNA  IGNITE
INUITS  IHAVEIT  DAGGER
NETPAY  TOYOTAS  SPENDS
```

3

```
ILIAC  AFTS  PUMA  IMACS
WANNA  GAZE  OREL  TARRY
IVANTHETERRIBLE  SRTAS
NANANANA  ARAB  INTENT
ARTHURCONANDOYLE
VSHAPES  TOOT  LOUR
ETON  AUTO  OMENS  QBS
NAPOLEONBONAPARTE  ULE
NYE  ACUTER  LTRS  SAIN
GTOS  HAIG  ATKINS
SAMUELTAYLORCOLERIDGE
PIUSXI  LEAP  OSIS
ARCH  ELAM  ADJOIN  ADD
TEK  ELVISAARONPRESLEY
EDS  TAINT  CBER  APSE
MASC  THOR  TOPTHIS
CHRISTOPHERREEVE
PUEBLO  RAIN  NEATIDEA
ROLLE  LAURENCEOLIVIER
AMOUR  ELLS  PERF  TENET
TOTES  OBIT  ROOF  ESTES
```

4

```
PRES  MOROS  GUN  MORK
AESOP  SAINT  ONESEASON
RAMBLINROSE  PASTELHUE
AMEBAS  STPAUL  TOOLATE
EYRE  EDNA  ONCE
SNERD  CANCERCURE  AGER
LAX  ACUTE  DIES  DEBONE
OPIATE  WAC  PSIS  BLOTS
TATLER  IRATE  ACCREDIT
EASE  LENO  ORO  ORE
OWNS  BALDINGPATE  BLED
NIM  SRS  GIRL  SWEE
TEAMMATE  CAVED  TIEBAR
ISSUE  OLEO  ESE  ENROBE
MESSED  SAME  TRADE  YEN
ELEC  OVEREXPOSE  GESTE
ALTI  COPA  SALE
STATUES  ANIMAL  SALAMI
LAMEBRAIN  RESUMESPEED
APPLESEED  ELITE  SORRY
BESS  DRY  DANZA  TOLL
```

5

```
BAGS  PRISON  SLOBS  RHEAS
OREO  CONTRA  EARLE  HELLO
MYOUTPUTISDOWNBUT  EASEL
BARRISTER  ARACE  STORAGE
ANGEL  RIO  AGE  BURST
YSER  MYINCOMEISUPITAKEA
TEEM  TRA  TOT  PACERS
POMPOUS  FEB  AORTA  THANT
SHORTPOSITION  TIME  ENER
ASNOT  RES  TATE  NANU  ESO
LATTE  ACE  FILL  IONA
MYEAR  CLASS  CLOWN  TRISH
XENA  LSTS  AAA  ARNIE
SAW  DUMA  OJOS  VIC  NIGER
AVOW  TERM  ONTHELONGBOND
MIRES  ORALE  IOS  COLADAS
BALBOA  IDA  LEO  SORE
ANDMYREVENUESTREAM  DCII
ABBIE  DNA  SUD  MEANT
CLOSEST  OLINS  AUTOPARTS
OUTTA  HASITSOWNCASHFLOW
SIREN  EZINE  AIDERS  TINA
TSARS  ROSES  READTO  ONER
```

6

```
MAN  SCALPS  ACTIII  COG
ELI  ALLSET  FLACON  ARR
NUT  BEAUTYPROTEST  REE
UMPIRE  ILL  MAP  RIDGE
INASTATEOFPROFUSION
ROCS  EEL  DWI  PADRONE
OAKUM  ADO  EEE  NEA
THELIBRARYOFPROGRESS
HURTLE  GAP  IANS  LOAF
ANA  ART  STE  RINGO
ABSENTMINDEDCONFESSOR
FACTO  ASI  DEO  DAS
BNAI  AILS  TAP  SEAMUS
GROSSNATIONALCONDUCT
LOS  MSS  LEA  TESLA
SKIAREA  NIN  ESS  LIAR
CONTESTANTWORKETHIC
OASES  HUE  ASH  REECHO
FLU  PROFESSIONBOX  ION
FAR  ONMEDS  ENROBE  TSE
SSE  THEUSA  REAPED  YES
```

7

```
ASSIST  SLED  SPITON
QUELQUECHOSE  HOOKNOSE
TDWATERHOUSE  OKCORRAL
SINGE  SIR  EMCEE  ISTO
SLEETY  HLMENCKEN
ABATE  FIE  AREOLAE
AMFM  CSLEWIS  SNOG  PTA
REGISTRY  NEDS  SUGAR
PROTEUS  LANCE  INAPTLY
OYER  PERK  NINOTCHKA
MCD  EZBAKEOVENS  IAN
CORNBREAD  EWER  TBAR
CHINESE  TAPER  FAUSTUS
ONCEA  CODE  BULLPENS
OSH  URDU  JREWING  CELT
STBARTS  GAG  IVANV
MXMISSILE  OLDSAW
ARUN  MINSK  TOO  BUGLE
YATITTLE  UNRESOLUTION
EYESORES  SECRETAGENTS
DEPART  SEAS  HISSAT
```

8

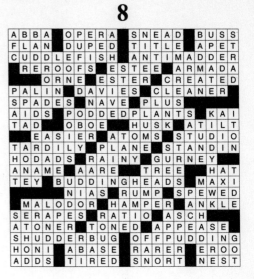

```
ABBA  OPERA  SNEAD  BUSS
FLAN  DUPED  TITLE  APET
CUDDLEFISH  ANTIMADDER
REROOFS  ESTEE  ARMADA
ORNE  ESTER  CREATED
PALIN  DAVIES  CLEANER
SPADES  NAVE  PLUS
AIDS  PODDEDPLANTS  KAI
TAD  OBOE  HUSK  ATILT
EASIER  ATOMS  STUDIO
TARDILY  PLANE  STANDIN
HODADS  RAINY  GURNEY
ANAME  AARE  TREE  HAT
TEY  BUDDINGHEADS  MAXI
NIAS  RUMP  SPEWED
MALODOR  HAMPER  ANKLE
SERAPES  RATIO  ASCH
ATONER  TONED  APPEASE
SHUDDERBUG  OFFPUDDING
HONI  ABASE  RARER  EROO
ADDS  TIRED  SNORT  NEST
```

9

```
LABEL  HASTE  BEEFS  MRE
ENURE  USURP  UNCUT  OER
IDONTLIKEYOURTONE  LPS
SAYSHITO  NETS  NESTEA
TAP  VINYL  AILMENT
ALF  LONESOMEDOVE  ANTZ
LEAF  ERAT  ONAROLL
ATLANTA  ADDICTS  SLAKE
MOSQUITOCOAST  TELAVIV
ONESIDED  BLOC  TODATE
IREST  AROAR
COOKIE  SCOT  SNAKEPIT
CAREERS  EBONYANDIVORY
STANS  TINYTIM  LEXICON
NOTAONE  ECCE  LUNA
EGGS  LOVINGCARESS  SSN
TOEHOLD  ARESO  EOS
HAZARD  ASTO  UPGRADES
ILE  DONTTOUCHTHATDIAL
CIS  ENEMY  NIMOY  OTERO
SET  REESE  DAMNS  FOUNT
```

10

```
PASTED  AWAKEN  ATTACHE
INCODE  CALICO  BRONZED
KNOWSFOURGNUS  MASTERY
EARN  TWAS  SEM  DEICES
ESO  ETHOS  RETEACH
ABC  BAREINNMINED  BRO
BRACER  POLENTA  ASIAN
EARLYISH  NGO  GRAMPS
DUDE  MISTRESS  ORNATE
FEDERICO  ATEALOT
AMY  MEATBUYCHANTS  ERS
POUTIER  APOSTATE
POLAND  GOPLACES  AWAY
ALEROS  ENO  CYNICISM
LABOR  BOONIES  ETHNIC
SHE  BORNETWOLOOS  DNA
ENLARGE  EELED  YAP
MEMOIR  ESA  AVES  ROPE
ABILENE  WRYBREDFLOWER
HASTIER  AMELIE  PAMELA
INTENSE  YENTAS  DWARFS
```

11

```
METS  STAFFS  PAD  HIM
HANOI  INDIAN  OLDJEANS
ANION  SUITCOMPLAINING
LUSTALITTLEBIT  YGOR
SALVIA  SYD  LAM  STYLI
LEE  SPA  INBED  EGAD
GATINSTYLE  SAG  OLE
DEEM  NACHOS  ASWANDAM
SEATAT  SHERA  RANSOM
ITSAJOB  IRK  FIG  XSOUT
ARIB  PURSESAIDES  ETNA
MENLO  LEM  TAC  SIOBHAN
GENTLE  FUNKY  PRYERS
HOTSTUFF  ODDLOT  WARM
UNH  ORR  RAYPERVIEW
TIED  FOCAL  EAN  HAP
STJOE  GAD  ISO  DRIVEN
ONLY  MISSINGCOUSINS
DRINKOFDISASTER  SKATE
JANEEYRE  NATANT  SERAC
SET  OON  SCAPES  ORYX
```

12

```
ALLPRO  RESAVE  TRIBAL
LTILES  MINIVAC  HORACE
MYFAVORITEMART  EDITED
ARTIE  ATARIS  OPS  STLO
NARZ  GATO  JEN  IAN
BATTLEOFBIN  RESTAIN
ALAS  MRLEE  MIX  LINGER
TOM  TYSONS  AEC  ESTATE
HOPIN  HET  ANNE  THEGAP
SPATULA  SEDATEST  LESS
STIRS  NOG  DIETS
ARCA  SPENGLER  DREAMUP
NODSAT  CARL  EVE  STASI
KALINE  AVA  ARETES  VIC
ARAGON  DEM  TIROS  PENA
UNUSUAL  TOGASPRINGS
MAG  KTS  SOHN  INEZ
OCHS  OHO  TEEMED  CAIRO
OTTAWA  BOTOFTHEBARREL
LEERED  IRONONS  SPRANG
ADRATE  TASERS  ASONIA
```

13

```
OSCAR ARMS INGE PERU
HOOVER TOIT NEOPHYTES
MYLIFE OGRE CATHARTIC
SAD INAMERICATHEYOUNG
CELEB TONI LSD
AREALWAYSREADY REDACT
KERR ETE MRX LAMINAR
ILE CRETAN DIME ISSUE
TIARA TOGIVETOTHOSE
ATLAST PELF AAA ONES
WHOAREOLDERTHAN
SABU PLO AURA UBOATS
THEMSELVESTHE ERNIE
ASABC BOSC SIGURD NEA
LINEAGE AHA UTE NATO
ENORME FULLBENEFITSOF
TSE EDAM NOCHE
THEIRINEXPERIENCE WOO
VERSATILE NINA USNEWS
PRIEDOPEN TUES SAMLET
GONE NERO EMMY WILDE
```

14

```
MONTERO WOWEDEM TERRA
AROUSER OOHLALA ALOES
DEBTOFASALESMAN HOOPS
AGUT CEDAR ALAMO TEE
MOTOROLA EXS YELLAT
ENS THERATOFKHAN EELS
SEM RONA ENACTS
SSGTS TBAR CARE ATSEA
APIP USEBOATHANDS PAS
FIVEONES COM DUSTERS
ACETIC SECURED RIVOLI
RUBELLA NUT ROASTPIG
ILE WELTCREATION ALEN
SERTA IBLE CAPP APERS
TRYSTS ADES HUE
ESTA POPULARMITTS DRY
UTOPIA ELM COSTFREE
REA FRANC PLIER LADS
ALBEE TAKEMYBRETTAWAY
ILONA ONEVOTE AVARICE
LAYER PARAPET TALENTS
```

15

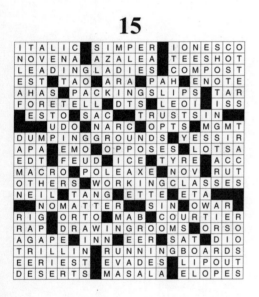

```
ITALIC SIMPER IONESCO
NOVENA AZALEA TEESHOT
LEADINGLADIES COMPOST
EST TAO ARA PAH ENOTE
AHAS PACKINGSLIPS TAR
FORETELL DTS LEOI ISS
ESTO SAC TRUSTSIN
UDO NARC OPTS MGMT
DUMPINGGROUNDS YESSIR
APA EMO OPPOSES LOTSA
EDT FEUD ICE TYRE ACC
MACRO POLEAXE NOV RUT
OTHERS WORKINGCLASSES
NEIL TANG ETTE ETA
NOMATTER SIN OWAR
RIG ORTO MAB COURTIER
RAP DRAWINGROOMS ORSO
AGAPE INN EER SAT DIO
TRILLIN RUNNINGBOARDS
EERIEST EVADES LIPOUT
DESERTS MASALA ELOPES
```

16

```
ATALOSS CROCI OCANADA
SHRIVEL ALTHO LOWERED
PENNAME RESAW DALLIED
SOOT IDOLS RELAX LAPS
GUYS DYES
MARG BESS OATS SLUE
GLORIA TIS EUP EMISMS
MAKEST EMOSTOF NASDAQ
ART ROSSANO ANT
GRATAE SNARLER TOEING
TENDER EARTED
EASILY VANESSA SMITES
VIP APOGEES EAN
ROSITA LARGERT ANLIFE
POWDER ORN AVA TOATEE
THEE KART IRES WONG
MEMO BETH
TOAD EMMET ATEIN FOPS
INRANGE NETWT LOLITAS
NUCLEAR TRADE LAYSOUT
ASSIGNS SONYS SHEKELS
```

17

```
HDTV USAF OBJ ROSEHIP
AREA PAIL NAE ACETONE
JOLLYMRROGERS STATUTE
ILLSAY CREPTUP AMUSER
SLYER MOIRA RIDS IRA
GOODMRDEEDS SNAG
CEREBRAL STINTS INGLE
ANOMIE AGA SWAMIS
ISAID BRANDMRX COPRA
RUSSE YOWEE BANDB
NETS MRINBETWEEN RUST
EASED RIPEN TABOO
CDROM MODELMRT EGBDF
SIMILE AMO STOLAF
AGREE DROPIT FINENESS
LAPS MYBOYMRBILL
ERE REEL MILNE ADAYS
SCALER EUGENIA IMFREE
MANIACS SPRINGMRCLEAN
ASUNDER PAS KLUM ATRA
NETZERO SSE SEGA TENT
```

18

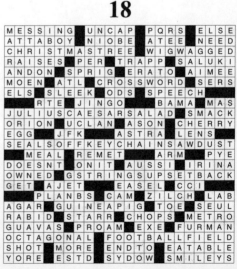

```
MESSING UNCAP PQRS ELSE
ATTABOY NIOBE ATEE NEED
CHRISTMASTREE WIGWAGGED
RAISES PER TRAPP SALUKI
ANDON SPRIG ERATO AIMEE
MOEN ATL CROSSWORD SERS
ELS SLEEK ODS SPEECH
RTE JINGO BAMA MAS
JULIUSCAESARSALAD SMACK
ORION UCLAN ASON CHERRY
EGG JFK ASTRA LENS
SEALSOFFKEYCHAINSAWDUST
MEAL REMET ARM PYE
DOESNT ONIT AUSSI IRINA
OWNED GSTRINGSUPSETBACK
GET AJET EASEL CCI
PLANBS CAM ZILCH LAB
AGAR GUINEAPIG TOE SEUL
RABID STARR CHOPS METRO
GUAVAS PROAM EXE FURMAN
OCTAGONAL FOOTBALLFIELD
SHOT MORE ENDTO EATABLE
YORE ESTD SYDOW SMILEYS
```

19

```
M A N T A S   R A C Y   W E B S   P U M A
O R E I D A   O L E O   I M A M   I N O N
R E V E A L   S I N G A P O R E S L I N G
P N E U M A T I C T I R E   A A L T O
H A R P   M I N E   S U G A R M A P L E
  N I L   S T O P I N   O R R I S
M E T R O S T A T I O N   V I S A   I T S
O R E O S   S P A S M   W E S T   A C H E
P U N C H C A R D S   E W E R   T E S S
E C O   O A T   I O N I A   I D O
S T R E W N   B R E W E R Y   A I M S A T
  U S A   R E S E W   S T U   C U E
P A A R   S C U D   M O T H E R L O D E
A N N O   T H I S   M O I R A   N O W I N
P I T   K A O S   B O W L I N G A L L E Y
A M I S H   R E L O A N   A O L
W A S H A T E R I A   E O N S   S O D A
  T E E N A   G R E E N P A S T U R E S
F O R E S T P R E S E R V E   I A M B U S
B R U T   E T U I   L I O N   P U M I C E
I S M S   R A G A   S K I S   S T A T E S
```

20

```
I C I E S T   K A N S A S   M A L A C H I
M O D E L A   I L O I L O   O N E S H O T
A M E R I C A N L I T E R   R A G T I M E
R E A   P O N D   S E E T H E   I C O N
E T T A S   E L M O   U N L I N K   E L I
T H E S H O W E R M U S T G O O N
  P O W   D E M I S E   U R A N U S
T L C   D E N T E   A M P S   V E R B A L
Y E A S   S O B E R S I S T E R   T R U E
P A U L O   D A D A S   S E R I O
E D G E R   E R S T   C O A T   A S T R O
  H A B L A   F O R G E   Y A H O O
F U T Z   O L I V E L O A F E R   N E A P
A L I E N S   N I N E   T A M I L   R M S
S E N S E I   A N G E L O   G E R
T E A   A N Y P O R T E R I N A S T O R M
  F E R G I E   T Y N E   S E P I A
O L I N   E T A L I I   U M P S   P S T
L I B E R A L   B U T T E R O F A J O K E
E M E R A L D   E N A B L E   C L O S E R
S A R O N G S   S A L E M S   S T E E D S
```

21

```
A E R O   C Z A R   I L O I L O   P U S S
T R E Y   L I N E   N O I D E A   E N T E
T O P S [ERG] E A N T   F O L I E S B [ERG] E R E
I D O T O O   I R O N S   S T A Y M A N
R E S E T   A C R E   S T P   S Y N [ERG] Y
E D E R   I S L E S   O A S   S T E
  B E T T [ERG] E T M O V I N G   N A P
  T H E Y S A Y   O O Z E D O U T   C M A
R H O D E S   A N T Z   S A T Y R S
O E R   O A K Y   H I V E S   N O F A T
A M I G O   P O L T [ERG] E I S T   G E O D E
D O Z E N   I D A H O   A L S O   R I O
M O O N E D   R O I L   B E A C O N
A R N   S I G N P O S T   I V O R I E S
P S T   F O U L W E A T H [ERG] E A R
  A H H   D N A   S H O E S   B A I T
  F L O O R   N Y C   C O P S   H U L C E
T A M A L E S   A L T A R   D U B L I N
E V [ERG] R E E N T R E E   E D G A R B [ERG] E N
A R E S   L A S E R S   A U E L   L E S E
M E R E   S P E A K S   U G L Y   E N T R
```

22

```
G O N G   S W A R M S   A C E D   T R I P
I S E E   L E N D E E   M A R E   R E M I
S U B S T A N D A R D   E P I C   O P A L
  T I N T   C O N N O T A T I O N S
R A D A R G U N S   N O D   U G H   I A N
A B E L E   P O O L A R E A   O R A N G E
P O S T D A T I N G   A D M I N I S T E R
T W I   S O R E A T   O V A L S
  C V I I   O I L   A L L O W E D
E X C O M M U N I C A T I O N   N I L E
A M A N A   N E M O   B A R K   B A S I N
S A N T   C O U N T E R B A L A N C E S
E S T R A D A   S K I   I N T O
  A T E S T   T I N E A R   N B A
P R O P O R T I O N   S U P E R V I S O R
H E L P M E   O N E L I T E R   O N I N E
A V E   I L A   G L O   S E A P L A N E S
S E M I C I R C U L A R   T A G S
E R I N   C O L A   D I S L O C A T I O N
R I S K   T S A R   E M I G R E   I O W A
S E S S   S E N D   R E C E S S   R U L E
```

23

```
G E L S   G I R L   B E S S   R A P I D S
E X A M   A D U E   R O A N   A C U M E N
E T T A   S O N A T A S T A N D S T I L L
  R E C U T   R U S   U F O   A N I
J A C K S O N I N T H E P U L P I T
A L A   E N I D   T E N   A S I M O V
B A R B S   V E N I S O N V I D I V I C I
B R E A   R E N O   T W O O N   E A T S
A G E D   E N T E R   S L A T Y   M E A
R E R E A D   S O N N E T P R O F I T S
  G R A S S   T I E   S T O L I
V I R G I N M A S O N R Y   U K A S E S
O N E   A T I M E   D A M U P   S N A P
I C A N   T O W A R   M O L E   C A R A
C A R I B B E A N S E A S O N   P O K E R
E N S T A R   O P E   C A S E   E D S
  P A R S O N F O R T H E C O U R S E
L E I   A V E   R I O   A N N I E
W A T C H Y O U R S T E P S O N   I V A N
O I N K E D   L O O T   P O R T   T E L E
E R A S E S   E S S O   S U E Y   E R S T
```

24

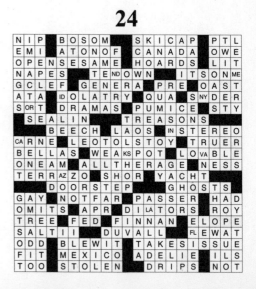

```
N I P   B O S O M   S K I C A P   P T L
E M I   A T O N O F   C A N A D A   O W E
O P E N S E S A M E   H O A R D S   L I T
N A P E S   T E [ND] O W N   I T S O N [ME]
G C L E F   G E N E R A   P R E   O A S T
A T A   I [D] O L A T R Y   Q U A   S [NY] D E R
S [OR] T   D R A M A S   P U M I C E   S T Y
  S E A L I N   T R E A S O N S
  B E E C H   L A O S   [IN] S T E R E O
[CA] R N E   L E O T O L S T O Y   T R U E R
B E L L A S   W E A [KS] P O T   L O [VA] B L E
O N E A M   A L L T H E R A G E   N E S S
T E R R [AZ] Z O   S H O R   Y A C H T
  D O O R S T E P   G H O S T S
G A Y   N O T F A R   P A S S E R   H A D
O M I T S   A P R   D I [LA] T O R S   R O Y
T R E E   F E D   F I N N A N   E L O P E
S A L T I I   D U V A L L   [FL] E W A T
O D D   B L E W I T   T A K E S I S S U E
F I T   M E X I C O   A D E L I E   I L S
T O O   S T O L E N   D R I P S   N O T
```

25

Puzzle 25

```
ATPEACE  JANDJ   FULCRA
BORSCHT  ELICIT  ALPHAS
ORESTES  SLEIGHDRAGONS
RESEAM CUE  ISEE   ALOU
TREX  LAOS  AWLS    LUC
SON  LAVA  PEEWEEWREATH
  TRIBAL  ILK   BTEAM
OASES  SPIELED  IASIMOV
PLOT  GTOS    INOR    ANE
OFFICE  RATTEDON  TAKEN
SIMEON  TIMELAG  DOREMI
SEISM  REDCROSS  AVISOS
URN   FERN   EONS    OTRO
MIDTERM  OUGHTNT  ASHEN
  IDEAS   SNO   WEENIE
LOBSTERCLAUS  OSSA   FOP
EXE   SKYE   SOTO   MIRE
AFRO  ETNA  MUD   BARRIE
DONNERTHEDEAD  SELLFOR
TRIUNE  EXALTS  ESTELLE
ODESSA  AMITY   MOSEYED
```

26

Puzzle 26

```
RCA  IDARE   UND   ACTFOR
LEAN  BARBER  LIE  EOSINE
SEVENSAMURAI  TNN  GUAVAS
TOES  OLIGARCHIES   INRE
ANNUALS   HAMMIEST   EEE
FOURSEASONS  ROOTS  DEANE
FREAK   ELATED  NIP  ORSON
SAS  SIXWEEKS  STEN  WRYLY
  AORTA   SACHS   MNOP
BROGUES  MAL  TAS  HAIRIER
RANAT  DREAMON  KERN  EMU
ODES  TENTOMIDNIGHT  ICON
NIH  TINA  LEADERS   BRETT
COOKING  TIN  SRA  BRAISES
  UOMO   WHATS   BOUTS
THROE  YARN  TWOJAKES  CIO
BOWLS  UTE  SPIRIT   MOOGS
AMISS  REEVE  EIGHTMENOUT
RET   QUIRKILY   RENEWAL
  HAUL  BILLMELATER  ENNE
CAYMAN  INE  HAPPYNEWYEAR
CHOPRA  RGS  ARGENT   HERS
CAUSES  DST  SNARE   YDS
```

27

Puzzle 27

```
MEDAL  ARIAS   SAFEHAVEN
AMINE  ROONE  ALEXANDRA
YESYOURXLNC  DOMINIONS
ARCTIC  YALL  SEATO   OOH
  HIST    EURO    IGN
BALI  BURNEDINFEG   ADAS
UCONN  NUS  ENGAGE   SERA
LNDGENERES   RANSOMER
BEE  REDACT  LOAN   PLATO
  AVRIL  ECARD  GAINON
SEALION  XPDNC  CORNDOG
ALLIES  SKIED   TOTHE
LICES  BTEN  AMARNA   IAM
ICANTSEE   UNKNOWNNTT
NITE  NARITA  EEE  KORAN
ETRE  LMNTARYMATH  REDS
  ASP   SOMA    SEAT
LAZ  EARTO  LBOS  ATHENA
ASSERTION  OBCTPROBLEM
MAKESROOM  AETNA  LAMIA
APPLEISLE  DROSS  LYONS
```

28

Puzzle 28

```
TESLA  AVON   CASS   ALIBI
OCEAN  BILE   IMHO   JOKES
SHAKO  BEAU   NOEL   ANNAL
SOLEDDOWNTHERIVER   ENA
  BEST   REMAKES   TWIN
ATTEST  ANIMALS  TILTED
HOOD   ARENA    YECCH
AFL  HOLEDONESNOSE   EEL
BULGARIA   STAR   STYNE
ERNST  GOESAPE   KUDOS
MADEDO  DOGLEGS  WAFFLE
ARIEL  AIRLINE   MOTTO
MATTE  TAME   BAKESALE
ALL  BOWLEDASBRASS   LOT
  IDAHO   WIRES   TENT
ANKARA  APRICOT  DREDGE
DEED   RETHINK   BIEN
RBI  GETTINGCOALEDFEET
OUTDO  AILS  AHME  CORKY
ILIAD  ILIE  LIME  AUGER
TASKS  LAPD  LOOP  PROSE
```

29

Puzzle 29

```
GLIDE  MAC  TIPPY   LAUDS
REDISTILL  ADORE   ERNIE
ANASTASIA  PEROTCHOICE
FALCONCARESSED   LASTED
  UMPS   EDITS   SEVE
TAPAS  SATIN   WAR    BSA
ERIN  BARRETTEMAVERICK
REN  WYLIE  OSCINE   ESAI
NAOMIJUDD  ELAN   STERN
  ALOT   GETAT  DEICES
DERIVEINRESTAURANTS
TRALEE  NOIRE    SOLO
OUTER  EARL  DIANELANE
AMEN  ANNALS  EBBED   REX
DURESSREHEARSALS   RISE
SPY  WHO  LEERY   TESTS
  LEON   METAL   FAST
ACHIER  DERIDEAPRICOTS
SOULTERRAIN  CLEOPATRA
ADLAI  DANCE  TENGALLON
PEACE  ABYSS  SET   NEEDS
```

Puzzle 30

```
SPEWS  OSIER   GIBB   OOPS
TOSIR  CADRE   OTRA   DRAT
ALLNIGHTERS  GUARDDUTY
  GLAREDAT   OPERAS
PROBATE   TIA   SENHORA
LINEN   STARSKY   TOOLED
STEAK  SLO  FAUST   EDGE
STARTINGPITCHER   SIN
APO  CAMEOUT   CASHEWS
TOWNCAR  DEN  DAM  ELITE
MONEYS  MUSCLES  BISTRO
ERWIN  FOP  HAG  SENECAN
HELIPAD  SERRATE   HRS
SOI  CLIENTSCASEFILE
LUGS  ALLIE  DTS  VIRGO
ASHPAN  SNIFTER  ETONS
PETITES   NAH  RAGTOPS
  EUCLID   TEENIDOL
HANDBRAKE  WISDOMTEETH
BRIO  EVER  ASSAD  IMAGO
OMAN  WEAN  SMOKE  TEPID
```

31

```
VNECK  TBONESTEAK  AONE
CONDE  HUBBAHUBBA  POEM
HOTSY  ERECTORSET  EZRA
INE HARPY HONES  TREVI
PERFORMS LETON  CHISEL
    ELIS  SOREN  TOAT
INBRED  EVER  WHATISIT
MOORS HARE  SHEL  FEAR
AREA NONE BATES  USAGE
CARRIESON  GYRATOR  LOX
   INITIALINITIALS
EDT SLENDER  KICKSTAND
BRETT STEAL EEKS  ACAD
ANNI USED  LOSS  ATRIA
YODELLED  MAIN  STEELY
    SOAS  TITLE  SAHL
OSBORN BADLY  BELLYRUB
ROUND MALTA SLATE  ANS
IDLE MILLENNIUM  TAMMI
NOGO AFTERTASTE  INBED
GMEN IFORMATION  CNOTE
```

32

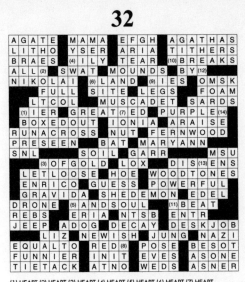

(1) HEART (2) HEART (3) HEART (4) HEART (5) HEART (6) HEART (7) HEART
(8) HEART (9) HEART (10) HEART (11) HEART (12) HEART (13) HEART (14) HEART

```
AGATE  MAMA  EFGH  AGATHAS
LITHO  YSER  ARIA  TITHERS
BRAES (4)ILY TEAR (10)BREAKS
ALL (2) SWAT MOUNDS BY (12)
NIKOLAI (6) LAND (9) IES OMSK
   FULL  SITE  LEGS  FOAM
   LTCOL  MUSCADET  SARDS
(1)IER GREAT(7)ED PURPLE(14)
BOXEDOUT  IONIA  ARAISE
RUNACROSS  NUT  FERNWOOD
PRESEEN  BAT  MARYANN
SNL  SOIL  GARR  MSU
(3)OFGOLD LOX DIS(13)ENS
LETLOOSE  HOE  WOODTONES
ENRICO  GUESS  POWERFUL
GRAVIDA  SHEDEMON  EDEL
DRONE (5)ANDSOUL (11)BEAT
REBS  ERIA  NTSB  ENTR
JEEP ADOG DECAY DESKJOB
LIZ NEWISH JUNG NAZI
EQUALTO RED(8) POSE BESOT
FUNNIER INIT EVES ASONE
TIETACK ATNO WEDS ASNER
```

33

```
TBONE  MUIR  AEONS  SLED
AARON  ATNO  RELEE  COPA
ETATS  REFS  GREATBRAIN
BITINGCROSBY  OPULENCE
ONECAR ORIOLE SPEE
   ERES  NOEND  SUNOCO
DEADLYSITIN VII  EULA
UNS STLO SHORTCIRCUS
RENEW SOON AIKMAN  HET
ARETHA SLAIN  ANTI
NOWYOUSEEITNOWYOUDONT
   MODE  LEACH  ERENOW
SHA PIRATE HEIL  NOTSO
SUNVISITORS ASEA  HIP
RANI  FAR  HUNTINGPERM
SCENEV BARON  SOIR
   ETAL HORSES DROWSE
AREYOUOK  ONEARMEDBAND
TITANLINES ATTA  ELSAS
ASTR TREAT TMAN  RETIE
TEED SEERS SESS  SMELL
```

34

```
FUNGO  CLOTS  DAFT  SPA
ONION  THELAW  ELLA  TON
EAGLE  MADAMIMADAM  END
   PEDDLES  INAROW  HWYS
BARB ANE BAERS  STOAT
BRIEFS FROM TAE  OPRAH
STARRS IONIZING  YETIS
   GAO ECO ONTOP  SILT
CCCVI ILK ERMA  ARPS
AURAL CDC MBA  CARLAS
STYRENE OSCAR SATIATE
ASSISI RAE ICU  INNIE
   TATA SNEE EAR OGDEN
FRAT SAWIN CTR  ONS
BELIE DESSERTS CAESAR
INGOT DAH CIAO  ELTORO
TANDY THROB NBA  ELAN
DAZS ALBEIT  CONTROL
ACE GREENGOBLIN ANISE
MAR EDNA ONSITE DANES
ERS ESTD READY  ALGAE
```

35

```
DITTO  ANTED  TRAC  ESPN
ONEAL  HEAVE  RAUL  GRIT
ONEBELOWPAR  UNDEROATH
FATS ERAS AGELIMIT
UTE LSAT TIETO  ENIGMA
SERBIA FOLLOWINGSUIT
   RAGWEEDS  STOMATA
BEFOREHAND VAGUE  VEL
ODIC IRS IAGO  AWARE
EDNABEST ADLIB  FRI
RANDOMHOUSEUNABRIDGED
   EDS ELISE CRAPGAME
ABYSS ANAT OKA  ELIE
DRU LORAN ABOVEBOARD
DASBOOT  DRONESON
OVERSUBSCRIBE  POSING
NOFAIR TOONS MAIN  MOO
   LEANONME MIME  AGRO
AFTERWARD  THELASTWORD
BOOS LIMO TOTES  MANIA
EXES SLYS EVERS  CREST
```

36

```
INFRA  BALI  RWE  CHEESE
COLOR  REINDEER  AORTAS
KNACKFORGROWINGPLANTS
   SAMEHERE  SOIL  ASE
AMCS COOT MAC  ATAT
SALAMI  TIVO  BANGLE
SPECIALFORCESSOLDIER
ALA SLURPEE MAUI  ARE
DENT MOPE MINT  CSPAN
   HARES  TEAS  EATING
DOCUMENTFORIMMIGRANTS
OROMEO APIN APODS
CLUBS HICS SOIR  HERB
SES PORT CARNAGE  PEE
SIGNALTODRIVEYOURCAR
SNOOPY RIAL  TRIODE
   AVES YET ERBE  STET
SOL OREM DISLOYAL
WHATTHEMOONISNTMADEOF
ANDREA LOWGRADE  CARLA
MODEST INN ESOS  KNEES
```

37

```
N CAR . THAI . ADEAD . MOAN
ROOM&BOARD . DOWN&DIRTY
INREBUTTAL . ABANDONEES
CONN . RAH . YEMEN . TOSEE
ONEDOLLAR . A&E . IKEA
HOT . RAU . ETTE . ARIDNESS
. DEPP . SHIVAREE . AWE
EMAILS . OPENERS . LARSEN
GINAS . NIB . FOP . HAYES
OXYGEN . TROAS . NAUSEATE
M&M . ACHES&PAINS . S&L
AMICABLE . SPECS . SAMPLE
NANNY . VCR . LAT . VAIOS
ITUNES . HERALDS . RENEWS
ACT . EPISODEI . MEDE
CHECKSIN . DORA . ADO . MAB
. RISK . R&R . NETINCOME
PATIO . BERET . NIA . REST
CROSSBRACE . ATALLCOSTS
BLACK&BLUE . CURDS&WHEY
SODO . BIKEL . TEMA . WEAL
```

38

```
BLAMES . SADCASE . CUERVO
RAMONE . CLERKED . ALLIED
EMBRACEABLEEWE . LEANTO
SELECTOR . TALENT . IGOR
TRENT . NIB . MAR . IRANI
. ESP . NOUS . PRETEND
SUBS . RIGHTONQUEUE . GIT
PRUSSIA . REDOUT . PUTTER
AGR . HEMO . RATA . SPORTY
TENNISSHOO . ARMS . MUS
. ENTAIL . TOUSLE
TNT . MODS . MOUNTAINDO
PROWAR . BETA . EDEL . OED
TATTLE . SATEEN . ENABLED
SPH . IDONTHAVETWO . RODS
PISCOPO . REMO . SAO
NTEST . BRA . ONA . DWARF
GAGA . SERAPE . GREENPEA
ANGLEE . RUNAROUNDSIOUX
INNEED . ATTRITE . ETERNE
LAUDED . SESTETS . RESTED
```

39

```
TWOS . OVENS . BOPS . UPBOW
HALO . BASIN . EDIT . PUPAE
ACDC . ALLBASSETSAREOFF
WOEISME . SPOTTY . DAREST
. EVANS . SLIT . BAIT
CRETE . SHUTTLECASSOCKS
LARYNX . INOIL . ANTE . HAT
ARIP . AURA . ENGR . WISE
META . XKE . PRATT . APACHE
PRUSSIA . SIESTAS . OSKAR
. SASSINGTHEBLUES
DORAG . EMIGRES . INTAILS
COOGAN . SPYON . CDC . IMIT
COVE . EMUS . DUEL . LIMA
ALE . OWAR . COEDS . ELINOR
BAREFACEDLASSIE . ANGST
. ANGE . RITT . PANDG
CRUSOE . PAPERY . TOYWITH
CULTURALMORASSES . ADAM
LINOS . DIAN . DEARE . LENO
INANE . MESS . AROSE . LAGS
```

40

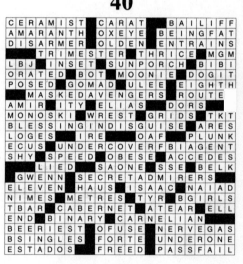

```
CERAMIST . CARAT . BAILIFF
AMARANTH . OXEYE . BEINGFAT
DISARMER . OLDEN . ENTRAINS
. TRIMESTER . THRICE . MGM
LBJ . INSET . SUNPORCH . BIBI
ORATED . BOT . MOONIE . DOGIT
POSED . GOMAD . ULEE . EIGHTH
. MASKEDAVENGERS . ROUTE
AMIR . ITY . ELIAS . DORS
MONOSKI . WREST . GRIDS . TKT
BLESSINGINDISGUISE . ARES
LOGES . IRE . OAF . PLUNK
ECUS . UNDERCOVERFBIAGENT
SHY . SPEED . OBESE . ACCEDES
. LIED . SAONE . SSE . BELK
GWENN . SECRETADMIRERS
ELEVEN . HAUS . ISAAC . NAIAD
NIMES . METRES . TYR . BGIRLS
TBAR . CABERNET . ATEAR . ELL
END . BINARY . CARNELIAN
BEERIEST . OFUSE . NERVEGAS
BSINGLES . FORTE . UNDERONE
ESTADOS . FREED . PASSFAIL
```

41

```
AGASP . ESTOP . MAITREDS
TOSIR . THEWEB . ONTHESEA
PLACECHEESEONTOSEESAW
ADM . TAE . KNEESOCK
RAISESLITCANDLE . LEGS
. TNT . ORATE . LUDENS
CDCASE . NES . THETAB . NEA
AERIE . FINAL . ANON . SELF
NAIR . HEATSUPTEAKETTLE
DTS . SAT . STER . TAI
WHISTLEJOLTSDOZINGCAT
. SAL . ASIF . CIR
TIPSOVERAQUARIUM . BODY
HMOS . ADOG . LEEDS . BIDES
AMI . CRUDES . OHO . ARREST
DINGHY . MANET . PET
. XTRA . FLOODSMOUSEHOLE
. INLIEUOF . SEZ . REX
BUILDABETTERMOUSETRAP
ARTLOVER . HECTOR . BOISE
GLOSSARY . SAVOY . YENTL
```

42

```
MAJOR . BUSLANE . IAMS . TMEN
ADOBE . ONEIRON . SWAK . HILO
LIKEFISHIFITS . MARIGOLDS
ONEARM . SEEOUT . STRAND
. HYATT . FRESHITSGOOD
ALE . TURKIC . EPA . OSAGE
LILAC . RAINES . INCASH . TRE
TRUTHINITSSUNDAYCLOTHES
SALOON . THEUSA . CARLO
. PRAM . TRAVAIL . WEAR
OBI . IRISH . ANECHOASKINGA
HORIZONTAL . CONTENTION
SHADOWTODANCE . PEETE . DDT
OREL . LABELER . ETES
. ERNIE . SAYIDO . EPILOG
THEDEIFICATIONOFREALITY
WON . EPINAL . MRKITE . DONOR
ORRIN . MLI . ESSENE . DEO
ANACTOFPEACE . NEARS
. GARBLE . NEWBIE . SALLIE
ONINYEARS . BEINGNOTDOING
DONS . SIKH . ALLGONE . OMEGA
ERGO . ELSE . GLEANER . NOSED
```

43

```
JOLT  TRAD  ETHER  ATBAY
ARIA  AUTO  NOISE  VIOLA
MARKSPITZ  JUNEPOINTER
SLEEPIN  IHOPE  ABASHED
   SING  NOYES  RETE
 FAINT  AGREE  VASELINE
DONNYOSMOND  JIBES  CUR
ERN  IFFY  DUEL  FIDO
AGES  GRAF  KENJENNINGS
RESTORER  JACKO  AINGE
  ARES  FORKS  PIKE
 MARIE  AILES  CELESTAS
MERVGRIFFIN  SRAS  TORO
ADEE  RATE  SPUR  RIO
SEE  PERCY  ETHELMERMAN
CALLEDIT  LAPEL  ANEEL
  ONIT  CESAR  BIGD
ATLANTA  HAITI  ELECTRA
FREDASTAIRE  CARLLEWIS
TOTEM  EARNS  ARGO  LACK
SWORE  DURST  LEST  LYES
```

44

```
 CREES  ICEAGES  SLAP
 HEAVE  FANWAVE  AWARE
MENSAWEARDEPARTMENTS
HOC  INNS  RUSE  GRIDDLE
ANKLES  CAIRO  SEA  RAT
WOEIS  THREEMENINATUBA
SCRATCHER  EXE  SLR
ELEM  ROWERS  HABITABLE
RED  FIRSTAIDAKIT  COAL
  PILES  FOILED  MITZI
CRANES  REFUGED  DANTES
HOSTA  TALIAS  LINGO
UPTO  INDIANAOCEAN  MAC
BEATINGIT  STRAIN  ELIA
  ARC  ACT  ACCEPTERS
AWALKINTHEPARKA  ROSSI
RET  SEE  NOBEL  JONSON
CATSHOW  TATA  ELON  PUG
ARIVERARUNSTHROUGHIT
ROLEX  RATTIER  CLEAT
ONAN  KISSERS  HEDDA
```

45

```
SASHED  ADAMS  ABE  GRIT
IMPALA  SADAT  BELGIANS
TURNSTOSTONE  ISSUANCE
ASIDE  SHA  SEALE  TNG
REGS  THESCARLETLETTER
 ATO  EER  ANSE  ARAT
SHOWHOWITSDONE  TENURE
TEL  ELEV  SLO  SATES
REALM  LANE  ENT  URE
ADFEE  ONEND  REPLACE
DEIS  SHOVEOVER  THEA
 RISESTO  BRIER  HEARD
ESO  EEK  TITO  ARNIE
 GUSTO  DIS  OLDS  DEL
HENSON  SIMPLEPLEASURE
ITBE  YEAS  AAA  ATH
PAINTINTOACORNER  AMBS
 ATE  GENRE  FAO  ATYOU
ELSINORE  MARLINLINEUP
STEADMAN  AGOAL  EDERLE
ADDL  EMS  SEEPS  VERSES
```

46

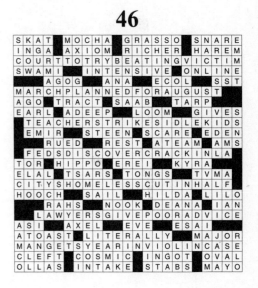

```
SKAT  MOCHA  GRASSO  SNARE
INGA  AXIOM  RICHER  HAREM
COURTTOTRYBEATINGVICTIM
SWAMI  INTENSIVE  ONLINE
 AGOG  ANA  ECOL  SST
MARCHPLANNEDFORAUGUST
AGO  TRACT  SAAB  TARP
EARL  ADEEP  LOOM  GIVES
TEACHERSTRIKESIDLEKIDS
EMIR  STEEN  SCARE  EDEN
 RUED  REST  ATEAM  AMS
FEDSDISCOVERCRACKINLA
TOR  HIPPO  EREI  KYRA
ELAL  TSARS  TONGS  TVMA
CITYSHOMELESSCUTINHALF
HOOCH  SAIL  HILDA  LILO
 RAHS  NOOK  DEANA  IAN
LAWYERSGIVEPOORADVICE
ASI  AXEL  EVE  ESAI
ATOAST  LITERALLY  MAJOR
MANGETSYEARINVIOLINCASE
CLEFT  COSMIC  INGOT  OVAL
OLLAS  INTAKE  STABS  MAYO
```

47

```
APSO  TRACHEA  HIHO  AFT
PLAX  NICHOLS  IDEA  LAO
BAREFOOTINTHEPORK  ELK
STAYAT  DOOR  MEASLE
 THEMERCHANTOFVENISON
 EAU  DAIS  MAWS
THEBURGERSOPERA  BEND
EUROPEAN  TIED  GEDDES
SMITTEN  BALL  MARGARET
HENSON  WURSTSIDESTORY
 GOAL  TREE
PORGYANDBISQUE  NUTMEG
AVERAGES  NOUN  FISHERY
RELACE  DRNO  PASSESON
 RANK  ABIESIRISHROAST
ASTI  TYKE  YET
CHITLINSOFALESSERGOD
CAVEIN  FLOE  WEARER
ODE  AHAMFORALLSEASONS
SOT  RAGU  STPETER  UNIV
TWO  STEM  SATIRES  POMP
```

48

```
AMINOR  SECANTS  BOOHOO
SATIRE  TAPROOT  ENRAPT
STOCKCHARACTER  TEASET
THREATENS  SLED  GLARE
  SNOW  SHOOTINGSTAR
LEAH  SOTTO  OTRAS
ABSORB  FRITOPIES  MARS
MASTEROFARTS  ANODAL
AYN  HORSY  ISLAM  EDINA
  MAAM  APIARY  SEEDY
WIZARDOFID  ACEOFCLUBS
AMEND  LOMEIN  SOIT
YALIE  URALS  CHILE  ORE
ORIANA  LIGHTNINGBUG
FIGS  BARBEDWIT  OTOOLE
  PIXAR  REAPS  LEER
COMPUTERICON  ARIL
ARIEL  LEGO  BARELYSEE
NINEPM  BALLPARKFIGURE
DOTTIE  IDIOTIC  ICEDIN
ONSETS  TENDSTO  THESKY
```

49

```
ACHE  OGPU  ARGOT  POSTS
CHUM  MIEN  MIRTH  ELIOT
CAMPAIGNPROMISE  CIGAR
ERA  STORIES  NERO  ONME
PINCH  LOLA  GAPS  HOS
TOPO  MODERNPROMETHEUS
STRODE  MAUI  COARSE
  EPISTLE  UNPEG  KLEES
EMT  JASONPRIESTLEY
GIZMO  ENGLUT  TOE  APSO
GREENE  GRO  IGO  STRUTS
SOLS  PUB  PAVANE  EDSEL
  SEASONPREMIERE  HMO
SAPID  DWELT  YAKUTSK
TRIAGE  IOUS  SHIISM
MANHATTANPROJECT  ONTO
OPS  ROWS  NELL  INPEN
RADS  NIPS  TIEBEAM  RRS
IHOPE  SILKSCREENPRINT
TOWER  TROOP  ERST  AZUR
ZENER  SEEDS  RTES  NEMO
```

50

```
LIBELS  HEWS  ASKS  THEM
ANORAK  ARIA  CHIA  HEMA
DANGCARROTS  TALLORDER
IFSO  TRICKDOWNTHEORY
DIA  BLEACH  ENL  MENSA
AXILLA  HAYES  SESSION
  SEMS  SODIUM  CNN
BREADANDBUTTERPICK
SEXT  SARAN  OAK  LOOSES
IPASS  KABUL  DISSENT
DEC  THETEMPOFDOOM  ARI
ENTREES  SCREW  OSLIN
STAINS  VHS  TULSA  SACK
  BOOGIEWOOGIEBUGBOY
MOT  URCHIN  RAFT
INHASTE  POSED  FOSSIL
SPORE  ALE  ERECTS  ANO
FAMILYSTYDINNER  ALTO
IPSOFACTO  THEJUNGBOOK
LEOS  LAIN  SOSA  SIENNA
ERNE  ENCS  ARTY  ALLSET
```